A BOUT

WITH

DOUBT!

A BOUT

WITH

DOUBT!

RESISTING THE TEMPTATION OF SILENT DISBELIEF

J. DREW SHEARD

HARRISON MASON PRESS

Xulon Harrison Mason Press
2301 Lucien Way #415
Maitland, FL 32751
407.339.4217
www.harrisonmasonpress.com

HARRISON MASON PRESS
A division of the Church Of God In Christ Publishing House

Paperback ISBN-13: 978-1-6628-3528-5
Ebook ISBN-13: 978-1-6628-3529-2

TABLE OF CONTENTS

Preface ix

Introduction xi

   1. Round One: A Bout with Crisis 1

   2. Round Two: A Bout with Self (The Past) 15

   3. Round Three: A Bout with The Chaldeans (People) . . . 31

   4. Round Four: A Bout with Justice 47

   5. Round Five: A Bout with New Thought (and
        New Age) 61

   6. Round Six: A Bout with Sin 71

   7. Round Seven: A Bout with Belief 81

   8. Round Eight: A Bout with Doubt 95

References 105

ACKNOWLEDGMENTS

I want to thank my Lord and Savior, Jesus Christ, for everything He is to me. Without God, I would be nothing. I thank Him for allowing me the opportunity to share in ministry.

To my wife and the love of my life: Karen Clark Sheard. For over 37 years, you have inspired, encouraged, and uplifted me. Your unconditional love and support are unwavering.

To my beautiful children: Kierra and J. Drew. I am incredibly proud of you both and am continually in awe of your God-given gifts. I extend much love to Jordan, my other son, and my wonderful grandchildren, Jacob and Kali Drew.

To my brother: Ethan, thank you for everything. Your profound strength and support will always be appreciated. Gwenda, my dear sister, I cherish you and my spectacular niece, Madison.

I extend sincere gratitude and a special remembrance to my parents, the late Bishop John H. Sheard, and Mother Willie Mae Sheard. I am grateful to God for the time I was honored to share with them and the many life lessons.

Thank you, Greater Emmanuel Institutional Church of God in Christ, the Michigan North Central Ecclesiastical Jurisdiction, and the Church of God in Christ, Inc., for allowing me to serve.

HABAKKUK 1:2; 2:1

"How long, O Lord, must I
call for help, but you do
not listen?
I will look to see what he
will say to me."

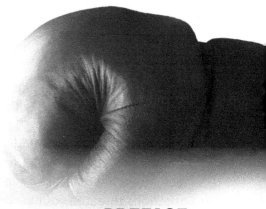

PREFACE

There has never been a time in my life when elevation was not imminent. From childhood, into adolescence, college life and adulthood, I have always been on track to climb higher and advance further—academically, professionally and spiritually. With every advancement, however, I gradually realized, there was no guaranteed immunity from heartbreak and disappointment. Contrary to popular belief, despite the adornments which attend the ecclesiastical office—please believe me—I too have had my dark seasons. I have walked in the valley of utter despair. Yes, I have seen, experienced and felt that desolate, lonely place where giving up seems the only recourse. As if it were only yesterday, I can remember being secluded behind an ICU curtain, a dismal veil of mental anguish, despondency and fear. Emotionally crippled. Clutching the tender hand of my dear wife, my whole world was caving in on me, hour by hour. It was an empty, isolated corner where I could detect not even a hint of sunlight. But just as the last ounce of my sanity seemingly began to slip away from me, the voice of God shook me and reminded me that I have already been invested with power over every attack of the enemy. I have already been given authority to call the enemy out and to shut him down! That's when the waterways of joy began to flood my spirit and drown out the voice of doubt. I was no longer intimidated. In my night season, God gave me a song and I cannot stop singing it.

From that moment, I embraced the charge to empower you, my brothers and sisters, with this assurance: When the pressure is on, when affliction has stricken the body, funds are desperately low, your household is falling apart on all four sides, hell hounds are on your trail, lies and deception are all up in your face, stress has overtaken every area of your life and unanswered questions threaten your very peace of mind—ultimately there is relief. However, your relief, your help, your deliverance and your recovery will have absolutely nothing to do with God's ability. But it will have everything to do with your faith. It's all about your faith! Because greater is He that is within you than he that is in the world.

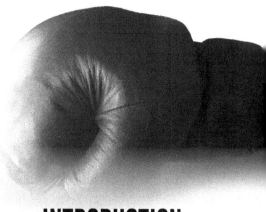

INTRODUCTION

G rowing up in a sanctified home, grounded in the principles of faith and holiness, strong emphasis was always placed upon choosing the right path. It was firmly embedded into every stage of my life and yet remains ingrained in my fondest memories. Like any other maturing young man, I've had my seasons of rainy days precipitated by my own lapses in judgement. But somehow, in the back of my mind, I knew for absolute certain, when it came down to that mental battle within, I was built to endure, fight back and win. Doubt was always hanging around, but thankfully, we never became friends. If the truth be told, I've watched that nasty little pest—doubt—turn the lives of many dear people to me completely inside out to the point where I can discern, close up or even at a distance, when someone has arrived at that critical crossroad of either walking, head on, into doubt or walking away.

What about you? Perhaps you have arrived at that crossroad. There are two paths to take. Suddenly you feel a warm nudge to follow the path of faith—the faith you have always known. Yet, with each step you take, there is also a whisper—a calm subtle buzz in your ear which gives off an air of uncertainty. It stirs up a pattern of second-guessing your convictions, your God and yourself: "Am I headed down the right path?" "Is there any light at the end of the tunnel?" "Is faith really the substance of things hoped for despite the absence of evidence?" Rather than brushing off this reality, this narrative will gladly revive what you already believe. It will rejuvenate what you have already testi-fied in His name. It will lead you down a long, though sometimes fragile, path which will bring you ultimately face to face with the time and place where you first believed and gave your life to Christ. For those who have yet to make that positive confession for Christ, no worries, Chapter Seven has you all covered.

This is an adventure! It is an expedition into the natural fear which accompanies unforeseen crisis and the necessary steps to survive it. It is a pilgrimage into your past failures minus the sting of shame. It is a sojourn into the reality that words really hurt and how "shaking off" the emotional damage is no maneuver for the faint of heart. This is a storyline which takes survey of how we process fairness. It places the spotlight on the portrayal of divine love, so powerful, so persuasive, that while we were yet without strength, "in due time Christ died for the ungodly" (Rom. 5:6). This is the believer's handbook of hope, help, healing and reassurance that doubt is a defeatable foe. As you turn each page, get ready to flip the script to discover that this race is not given to the swift, nor to the strong, but it's given to the one who keeps pressing on. Don't get caught up in pointless debates. Don't get distracted. Don't get sidetracked. Don't get turned around. Stay encouraged. Because when it's all over, have no doubt, you will surely win!

Pastors, evangelists, soul-winners, stock brokers, frontline workers, athletes, railroad conductors, engineers, homemakers, foreign missionaries, husbands, wives, singles, divorcees, mili-tary, seniors, millennials and baby boomers: If you can stay the course and embrace the challenge ahead, you will, at last, come to the place where you must admit that your steps have been ordered by the Lord, your life is groomed for greatness, your future is destined for deliverance and your calling is pre-ordained for God's glory. See your life story unfold through the landscape of Habakkuk on his watchtower. Experience the thrill of tram-pling over your doubts like a true champion. Speak up and ask questions without the torment of personal guilt. It's a crossroad. It's a decisive hour. It's a defining moment and for the first time ever, your opponent, doubt, has no idea what it's up against.

However, not like before. This time, your steady hand, swift feet and devoted prayer life will position you with the endurance to forget the problems of your past and press towards the mark for the prize of the high calling of God in Christ Jesus. Your prize awaits you.

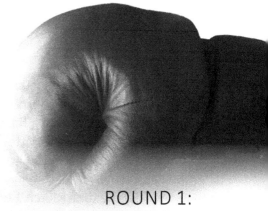

A BOUT WITH CRISIS

The Year 2020 came in with a bang. It was a bitter, harsh and brutal January. Trouble was everywhere. A Houston explosion had damaged nearly 200 homes. Major businesses were declaring bankruptcy. Killings by police were accelerating from Denver to Baltimore. Protests were disrupting the heartbeat of New York City. Tornadoes were rippling across the Everglades. It was a rough ride. News of the tragic helicopter crash killing NBA legend Kobe Bryant along with his 13-year-old daughter Gianna and seven others sent shockwaves across Los Angeles and the world. Conspiracy theories were on the rampage. Things were starting to spin out of control. Tensions were rising. Front page news had assumed an almost apocalyptic tone. The impeachment of the nation's 45th President was convening in the Senate. We had not seen such a whirlwind of drama on Capitol Hill since the spectacle of Watergate. And yet, on January 30, 2020—the most unforeseen, unforgettable event of our lifetime was about to hit. Flashing across every mainstream news outlet—BREAKING NEWS: The World Health Organization officially declares a Public Health Emergency of International Concern regarding COVID-19. COVID-19? Never heard of it. It took no time for us to make the unwelcome acquaintance with this acute, respiratory illness caused by a novel coronavirus.

Over the next 40 days, not unlike the people in the days of Noah, there was a silent panic growing in the air, hanging over every pocket of society: schools, businesses, restaurants, churches, public transportation; even the normalcy of walking down the street. It was a haze of uncertainty over what was to come. Doom? Despair? Utter destruction? While stockpiles of household goods accumulated in homes, leaving Supermarket shelves virtually bare, the instant panic swiftly assumed a life of its own. By the time March 11, 2020 rolled around, the pandemic was a full-blown reality—ultimately becoming one of the dead-liest pandemics in history. Between the around-the-clock news reports of confirmed cases, quarantine mandates and the com-plete shut- down of life as we knew it, there emerged the simul-taneous outbreak of questions. One after another: Is the world coming to an end? Is God's judgement being poured out on us? Is this the beginning of the end times? And more personally, am I being punished for something I have done?

Here we go. This is precisely how doubt gains its pulse. This is how it slowly morphs into an intimidating bully: by pushing your weak buttons during your weak seasons. It nudges you to inhale more doubt and exhale more panic. It keeps at you until you develop a habit of doubting. This unhealthy tendency only serves to obstruct your spiritual airways from indulging the prom-ises of God. It overreacts to the crisis at hand, stifling your ability to hear the Word of the Lord, which has already insisted that He is "striding ahead of you. He is right there with you. He won't let you down; He won't leave you." (Deuteronomy 31:6). Never.

Less than 365 days later came the roll-out of emergency vaccines. Fear moved in like a sudden Nor'easter. Immediately, there was anxiety, dismay and trepidation over the suggestion that the vaccine would mean falling victim to the "mark of the Beast." To be true to our theology, no true believer should be living in fear of such a mark nor such a beast—only unbelievers. By the time "the beast" arrives on the scene to wreak havoc, we will have already been snatched out of the way. We will be marked absent—nowhere on earth to be found. Gone. For at the appointed time, we will be "caught up together with them in the clouds to meet the Lord in the air" (1 Thess. 4:17). Place a book-mark here. We will circle back to this glorious thought, since it

Or cry out to you, 'Violence!' but you do not save?" He looks around and is less than thrilled by what he sees. The Chaldeans— this ruling class of Babylon, a terrifying presence, have gained dominion over Judah. To some, they are Babylonians nicknamed Chaldeans. To others, they are Chaldeans nicknamed Babylonians. Either way, they are an annoying tribe of troublemakers from the southern part of Babylon and they are a pain in Habakkuk's left side. They keep something going all of the time, and they do not know when to quit. They are relentless idolators whose ungodly influence is corporate, contaminated, calculated and deliberate. On top of that, God will use—of all people—these vicious and idolatrous Babylonians to judge His own people, "For, lo, I raise up the Chaldeans, that bitter and hasty nation, which shall march through the breadth of the land, to possess the dwelling places that are not theirs."

This presents an immediate crisis for Habakkuk. He is watching all of this unfold before his eyes and can hardly believe what he sees. In fact, at the root of his questions is one critical issue: Fairness. Through his eyes, the wicked surrounding the righteous is not only unreasonable, but unjust. Even worse, the wicked seem to be getting away with it. However, the prophet is bringing his tough questions directly to God. No sidebars. No off-the-record murmuring. He goes directly to God and gets straight to the point. His burden of prophecy is far too heavy to vent to any other man or fellow prophet. The task is upon him. It is his task to proclaim the Lord God as the one-and-only, divine protector of His people. It is his task to reinforce that God will sustain all those who trust in Him. And to repeat it, over and over, as needed— God will sustain all those who trust in Him.

Where does he end up? He ends up reminding himself of who he is. Who is he? He is a professional prophet, called of God and assigned the task of crying aloud unto Judah. While most of the Old Testament prophets spoke with certainty, "thus saith the Lord," Habakkuk, like Jeremiah, dared to ask "Why?" He was a revolutionary of his time. He was progressive—relentless in his pursuit to carry out the burden of the Lord's work. You can hear him raising these questions as early as 605 B.C., shortly before Nebuchadnezzar first invaded Judah. Consequently, his name means "embracer" symbolizing his "wrestling with God." Habakkuk is therefore prepared to embrace "the philosophical problems of the nation." Expressing neither judgement nor defense, he possesses a deep understanding of his fellow citizens' dilemma. He is tapped-in to their weak position. He feels their pressure. At the same time, he holds a high concept of the ideal life: work, industry, and the enjoyment of fellowship with the Lord based on equity and justice. One scholar remarked, "Habakkuk had a keen insight into the wickedness of his people and a thorough conviction of the only possible cure, which was faith in the promised Redeemer."

Nevertheless, in this dialogue, the prophet raises a timely problem. No sooner than he is introduced to us in his first chapter, he is pleading and supplicating, yearning to know just how long this will continue to go on. Without even taking a breath, he further points out to the Lord that "the law is paralyzed, and justice never prevails." Or does it? Has God actually forgotten the righteous and ceased to care? Not unlike today, Habakkuk lived during a time when lies, vanity, pride, arrogance and injustice prevailed. This was a deep-rooted issue. It was an ongoing problem, and year after year, Habakkuk cried out to the Lord over the inequity of the land without the consolation of any explanation. Stay with me.

While awaiting his answer, and from the tone of his aggravation, the second feature of Habakkuk's prophetic character is revealed. We already know he hardly fit the mold of Old Testament prophets. He was anything but traditional. But from here, we can further conclude that when it came to the fulfillment of his ministry, he flatly refused to conform to the status quo. Bravo for him! For as true believers, prophets and priests of these troubling times, perplexed by one crisis after another, confronted by the audacity of doubt, we must *work out* ways to *stand out!* If we expect to achieve effective ministry that meets the needs of this starving generation, we cannot be conformists. Our witness to the nations must look, feel, sound, behave and operate in a way it previously never has. For a sneak preview, this means fewer demands yet more faith-driven questions: "God, what are you doing?" linked with "Whatever is going on, I'm trusting You to bring me out alright." At the same time, this new, uncustomary look, feel, sound and behavior must rise above the trembling fear that questioning God is irreverent, out-of-line or even blasphemy. Over time, I have learned and embraced the fact that God welcomes us asking—so long as we are asking *right*.

On the Third Sunday in March 2020, just before the pandemic took a real stranglehold on the City of Detroit, I closed Greater Emmanuel. This was an especially bold move since all the members know how much I love to have Church. However, I felt God leading me in this direction. Our church remained closed for the next 16 months. I did not understand it. I did not want to do it, but I felt the leading of the Lord. This decision caused me to seek other ways to reach our membership and other people as well. It caused me to become more innovative as far as social media is concerned. As a result, our church has grown exponentially through social media platforms and God has continued to increase not only the membership but our finances as well.

Thank God there were no COVID-related deaths in our church and because of this, my faith in God has become even stronger. For those 16 long months, seeking God was my only recourse. Like never before, I can appreciate how James points out, especially in the midst of wars and fights, "you do not have because you do not ask. You ask and do not receive, because you ask amiss." Beware the pitfall of asking out of turn. This way, you will avoid becoming entangled in the frustration of feeling ignored by God as did Habakkuk.

Crisis is inevitable, but again, you are not alone. You belong to the same club as Abraham and the patriarchs. Abraham's crisis was scheduled at Mount Moriah. Technically, God's command to him seemed simple, at least ceremonially: "Take now thy son, thine only son Isaac, whom thou lovest, and get thee into the land of Moriah; and offer him there for a burnt offering upon one of the mountains which I will tell thee of." Be that as it may, the depth of Abraham's invisible turmoil must have been unbearable at best. How could this possibly be fair? If you listen carefully, despite the depth of his silent anguish, it could not silence his testimony (Gen. 22:5). Something mighty was at work within him. There was no doubt in his heart. No bitterness. No resentment. No protest. He and his son, he insisted, will go up into the mountain together and they *both* will return from the mountain together. No bout. No doubt. How was this possible? Had God already revealed the ram in the thicket to him? Of course not. Abraham purely, emphatically and unconditionally believed God! His resume of faith, at this point in his life, was flourishing, one test after another—with flying colors! Keep in mind, he had already survived the mid-life crisis of standing in the middle of his wife's wrath upon her Egyptian bondwoman with whom he had fathered a son. The argument then could be made: At least he didn't have to deal with the Chaldeans, as did Habakkuk. Not so fast. Scripture clearly indicates that Abraham was born and spent his childhood in Ur of the Chaldees, a prominent Sumerian city on the western Euphrates River. So, from day one, Abraham was all too acquainted with Chaldean drama. In fact, with all probability, Habakkuk is from the Tribe of Simeon, and as such, a direct descendant of Abraham— which follows naturally that there would be easily detectable traces of "faithfulness" in his DNA.

Whether he realizes it or not, Habakkuk is already cut out to manage this crisis playing out before his eyes. By the same measure, whether you realize it or not, you too have already been given the authority to step into the ring and take it on—one move at a time—one phase at a time.

Phase One: *Pre-Crisis*. As a starting point, you want to get ahead of the crisis, to be deliberate and proactive. As a rule, always prepare for war time during peacetime. Batten down the hatches. Prepare for the worst of conditions while believing God to command absolute order out of total chaos just as He did in the beginning by the movement of the Holy Ghost (Genesis 1:2). Brace yourself for a shock (Habakkuk 1:5). Before you get pulled in, see yourself coming out. Before high tide hits, see yourself landing safely on shore. Before you slip and lose your grip, hold to God's unchanging hand (Isaiah 41:10). Before the strong winds rip through the land, pack your bags and take refuge under the shadow of His wings (Psalm 57:1). Turn your shovels into swords, and while you are at it, throw out your chest and say, "I'm tough, I'm a fighter" (Joel 3:10). Though Habakkuk's bout with doubt is perplexing on the surface and comes across as whining, in his heart, he already knows that God will not leave His children trapped helplessly in crisis. The righteous will not be ultimately swallowed up along with the wicked. Let me say it like this, God's going to save you from embarrassment. I need you to know that the devil's ultimate objective is to destroy the people of God and put them to an open shame. That means you. Every chance he gets along the way, he intends to embarrass you. But be patient. Be still. Don't waver. Don't bend. Hang in there. When things get out of control, that's a clear indication that it may be time for you to step aside and let God step in on your behalf—and He will.

Phase 2: *Mid-Crisis: Once the crisis actually hits.* The crisis of his people's oppression at the hands of the Babylonians moves Habakkuk to release a cry unto God. He cries out to God by literally reciting the long litany of His mighty acts all the way back to the Exodus when God delivered His people out of the land of Egypt:

> You went forth for the salvation of Your people,
> For the salvation of Your anointed.
> You smashed the head of the house of evil.
> To uncover him from foot to neck. Selah.
>
> You pierced with his own arrows.
> The head of his leaders.
> They stormed in to scatter us;
> Their arrogance was like those
> Who devour the oppressed in secret.
>
> You trampled on the sea with Your horses,
> On the foam of many waters.
> –(Habakkuk 3:13-15).

Alive, quick and powerful—this is what it means to navigate acute crisis. It means to stay the course. Do not ever lose sight of Who is ultimately steering the vessel. Once that storm makes landfall, you will have no control over the direction, the intensity nor the speed of the high winds. None. They will blow away roof-tops and rip through baseboards, but they will never destroy your foundation. Your foundation is your faith. No need to slip into denial, you already know what to expect. Don't you? Of course you do. "Look at the nations and watch—and be utterly amazed. For I am going to do something in your days that you would not believe, even if you were told" (Habakkuk 1:5).

Finally, **Phase 3**: *Post-Crisis.* Assess the damage. Make the necessary repairs so you can move on. You will discover a whole new world of joy by employing the 2 Corinthians 4:8-9 model to assess the damage. It is splendidly paired up with a praise of thanksgiving for what could have been but was not:

> We are troubled on every side, (the damage),
> yet not distressed (God be praised!)
> We are perplexed (the damage),
> but not in despair (God be praised!)
> We are persecuted (the damage),
> but not forsaken (God be praised!)
> We are cast down (the damage),
> but not destroyed (God be praised!)

Assessing the damage means pulling out your best praise! It means keeping close watch of the time. Do not become caught unprepared in the eye of the storm and walk away permanently damaged. Walk through. Come through. Do not put it off another day. Do it *in* time and *on* time.

Perhaps just in time, before he recklessly abandons his iden-tity, Habakkuk ends up coming into a firm, unshakable faith by grappling with these tough questions! This is your blueprint—Facing your questions head-on. Looking them square in the eye and believing beyond a doubt that there is surely, unquestion-ably, a God in heaven Who will answer. Yes, I say, God in heaven will surely answer! This is the silver lining that runs from generation to generation, from faith to faith, from redemption to redemption and from glory to glory. Therefore, right off the top, the puzzle is solved—faith and doubt simply cannot ever co-exist.

Doubt is not your friend. It never can be. It is vindictive and conniving. It is vengeful and hypocritical. It is spiteful and manipulative. It is malicious and destructive. You deserve better. Just so long as you, like Habakkuk, go the extra mile to remind yourself who you really are: "You are a chosen generation, a royal priesthood, a holy nation, His own special people, that you may proclaim the praises of Him Who called you out of darkness into His marvelous light" (1 Peter 2:9). These privileges are impossible when you are in cahoots with doubt. Doubt is devious and controlling. Doubt sets up roadblocks to Damascus so that your eyes are never fully opened. Doubt is the ultimate public advocate of perceived unfairness. It dances across the canvass, applying brushstrokes until a life-size portrait of favoritism, negligence and wrongdoing is all you see. Doubt is exhausting. It drains you. It saps all of your energy and leaves your service, your worship, and the cultivation of your gifts depleted. Doubt, left unchecked, will stunt your spiritual growth. Doubt will undermine your ability to look back and rejoice at how God brought you through this season of crisis.

In fact, looking back, from the very first confirmed case of COVID-19 in December 2019 to the Public Emergency Announcement less than a month later, nothing—absolutely nothing— could have prepared us for what was to come. God knew all along. With our eyes pried open by the activity of faith, we too shall be able to see the impossible, survive the inconceivable and walk away without a scratch. COVID-19 is not the first health crisis to afflict the land and it definitely will not be the last. Scripture records a long-winded list of plagues and infirmities: blindness, fevers, leprosy, intestinal worms, paralysis, epilepsy and the list goes on. From this series of afflictions, we must remain steered in the right direction. We must maintain an up-front perspective that points us—not to the crisis at hand—but to the crisis to come. That is, the Supreme Crisis. The Supreme

Crisis for all humanity will be the crisis of The Last Judgement. The Word of God provides only one escape route. Our prayer lives, our fasting and personal consecration must meet the mark. No longer can we afford to hit and miss. This level of crisis preparation consummated through our personal confession of Jesus Christ as Lord and Savior, from day to day, from season to season, will spare us the doom of the last judgement. Remember, from the moment of the first trumpet sound, we will be nowhere to be found. We will be taken away, raised up and literally caught up in the first resurrection. "For the Lord himself shall descend from heaven with a shout, with the voice of the archangel, and with the trump of God: and the dead in Christ shall rise first: Then we which are alive and remain shall be caught up together with them in the clouds, to meet the Lord in the air: and so shall we ever be with the Lord" (1 Thess. 4:16-17). Do not allow yourself to be carried away by the chatter of the Chaldeans. Keep your ears in tune with that sudden sound from heaven (Acts 2:2). Do not allow your faith to be infected by the disease of doubt. Too much is at stake.

No one will think any less of you if you take your eyes off the unfairness swarming around you and fix your eyes on Jesus, the author and finisher of your faith. The One Who, for the joy that was set before Him—the joy of your ultimate salvation—endured the cross, despising the shame, and is set at the right hand of the throne of God. He is right there to intercede for you and to furnish the miracle of satisfying your tough questions. And if you can pull together the faith to ask and believe, just as sure as He will bring the captives of Judah back to Jerusalem, He will answer you. Loud and clear, Habakkuk, receives the first installment of his answer from the Lord in verse 5: "Look at the nations and watch—and be utterly amazed. For I am going to do something in your days that you would not believe, even if you were told."

Meanwhile, although this is only Round One, this is actually the perfect time to pull out your jab on your opponent: Doubt. The purpose of a jab is to block your opponent from getting too close. To pull off this move, come out with your less-dominant hand, with both hands fisted up near your face. Most importantly, your knees should be slightly bent. Once your hands are up and your knees are bent, the round is yours and your opponent—doubt—is already defeated. Just keep your hands lifted and your knees bent!

I cannot implore you enough to stay on your knees, hands up, looking up! Put on the new man, who has been created by God in righteousness and in the purity of the truth. Keep it on and wear it like a badge! When all is said and done, "many are the afflictions of the righteous: but the Lord delivers him out of them all."

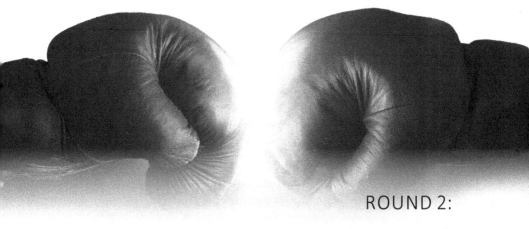

ROUND 2:

A BOUT WITH SELF (THE PAST)

Quiet on the set. Everyone settle into place. Take your seats. No walking. Pay close attention, because though you may be silently waiting alongside Habakkuk to see what exactly God will do, your Heavenly Father is waiting to see what exactly *you* plan to do. Are you planning to chase after His promises or are you carving out your own plans? Whatever your intentions, Jeremiah, who had plenty to say during the time of Babylonian captivity, relays an important reminder: "For I know the thoughts that I think toward you, saith the Lord, thoughts of peace, and not of evil, to give you an expected end" (Jeremiah 29:11).

To provide a framework for moving ahead with your future, in her book *13 Things Mentally Strong People Don't Do*, college psychology instructor Amy Morin includes a chapter about the dangers of dwelling on the past. She writes, "You can't be your strongest self when your brain is preoccupied with prior mistakes, past hurts, and nagging regret." She explains further, "Although a certain amount of self-reflection can, of course, be healthy for you, sometimes to become your strongest self, you need to be able to focus on the present. Looking backward makes it impossible to enjoy what's going on around you right now, and it prevents you from making the future as good as it can be."

This is a personal matter. Therefore, as you cultivate your personal walk with your personal Savior, never underestimate your personal worth in God's eyes. Neither should you ever

15

downplay your value among His sons and daughters. You are, hands down, His crowning masterpiece. By default, it is only a matter of time before you emerge as the standout one and only you! Best expressed, "The entire universe is standing on tiptoe, yearning to see the unveiling of God's glorious sons and daughters!" Not to mention "with eager expectation, all creation longs for freedom from its slavery to decay and to experience with us the wonderful freedom coming to God's children." (Romans 8:19-21). Here you have it: Your high-definition snapshot of what it means to be rescued from the slavery of your yesterday and transported into the safety of a new life that claims no personal perfection, but relinquishes the chains of the past, stamps out all doubt and looks forward to the inner man being renewed daily. It all belongs to you. Don't you see? The precise moment when all self-doubt is extinguished and the real you shows up, everyone will know it! Chaldeans and all.

Yes, the whole creation is awaiting the preview of the distinctive new you! How exhausted you must be by now, constantly chasing after your past, persecuting yourself over issues already settled at Calvary once and for all. How much of your emotional sanity has been depleted by struggling and scraping together the means to pay off a debt which has already been paid in full on the Cross? Loud and clear, the Scripture maintains, "There is therefore now no condemnation to them which are in Christ Jesus, who walk not after the flesh, but after the Spirit" (Romans 8:1). Do not get it twisted: Your past failures do not constitute your ultimate identity. Your failures will never triumph over your faith. Never. You are a sold-out, baptized believer whose footsteps have been ordered by the very God Who is able to do "exceeding abundantly above all we could ever ask or think according to the power that works within us" (Ephesians 3:20).

Tap into the power, wake up your faith and deal yet another blow to the spirit of doubt. Raw and uncut, sin's definition is "to miss the mark." We have all, from time to time, missed the mark, for all have sinned–intentionally, unintentionally and by our very nature. We were conceived in sin, all of us (Psalm 51:5).

This is precisely where doubt sneaks in, prompting you to question whether or not you are truly saved and if eternal life is in fact yours, without question or concern. You can go ahead and turn a deaf ear to these doubts. As a confessed believer, eternal security is already yours. Basically, eternal security is like an insurance policy, signed and sealed in the Blood of Jesus. So far, no better description of eternal security has been given than John's: "And I give unto them eternal life; and they shall never perish, neither shall any man pluck them out of my hand" (John 10:28). Paul however, drives the point all the way home: "Who shall separate us from the love of Christ? Shall tribulation, or distress, or persecution, or famine, or nakedness, or peril, or sword? As it is written, For thy sake we are killed all the day long; we are accounted as sheep for the slaughter. Nay, in all these things we are more than conquerors through him that loved us. For I am persuaded, that neither death, nor life, nor angels, nor principalities, nor powers, nor things present, nor things to come, Nor height, nor depth, nor any other creature, shall be able to separate us from the love of God, which is in Christ Jesus our Lord" (Romans 8:35-39).

Not everyone has this security. There are those who yearn—literally ache—for consolation. They immerse themselves in honorable, highly commendable works to compensate for their unconfessed sin—and worse—their outstanding confession of Jesus Christ as their Lord and Savior. They take to the streets and feed the homeless. They advocate legislation for funding women's shelters. They volunteer at soup kitchens. They build resources to combat poverty. They launch campaigns to save the environment and take a firm stand for animal rights. They walk for Leukemia, run for Parkinson's and march for Wounded Warriors. All the while, they are desperate to earn the Lord's pat on the back down the road, being miserable within, unable to embrace the free grace that saves through faith "not of works, lest any man should boast" (Ephesians 2:9). This sets a dangerous trap. Relying on your works alone only releases doubt to run loose on a fun filled playground with all the bell and whistles. It only helps along the plot to deter God's big plans for your future.

The last thing you need at this point in your life is for the fulfillment of these big plans to be thwarted by the unchecked audacity of doubt. Go back and read it again "There is therefore now no condemnation to those who are in Christ Jesus, who do not walk according to the flesh, but according to the Spirit. For the law of the Spirit of life in Christ Jesus has made me free from the law of sin and death." These are not plans or promises with an unclear outcome; these are plans with an "expected end." Of course, there will be hazards along the way, but no dead ends. There are no detours to lead you around in circles; only the guiding hand of God Whom you trust with all of your heart to gently bring you to your destination of ultimate victory. You will be forced along the way to take the service road, but only for testing. Trials are already worked into the trail.

Surely by now you can assess the difference between a trial and a train wreck. Right? Dr. Roger Barrier explains, "The purpose of trials is to refine our lives and leave us with a purer, stronger faith, as well as a character that God can bless and use. 'These have come so that the proven genuineness of your faith—of greater worth than gold, which perishes even though refined by fire—may result in praise, glory and honor when Jesus Christ is revealed' (1 Peter 1:7). The result of trials is that, over time, we begin to look more and more like Jesus." God will allow trials to come (and go) to perfect your molding process by His hands. The rule is simple: God's hand is at work in the midst of your trial until the trial has ended. A train wreck, on the other hand, is when your past creeps upon you like a rattlesnake, trips you up and gloats in seeing you flat on your face. And the only reason it takes so long for you to get back up is because you somehow allowed doubt to invalidate your future by entertaining unwelcome reminders from your past. This is what is casually known as "playing dirty." But now, you are too clean for that! Doubt will ring up the "old man" and conveniently nudge you to toss yourself into the same pool with those who cannot inherit the kingdom of God, including fornicators, idolaters, adulterers, effeminate, abusers of themselves with mankind; thieves, covetous, drunkards, revilers, extortioners, none of whom shall inherit the kingdom of God" (1 Cor. 6:9-10). But hold your head up. Because the wonderful fact remains, "such were some of you: but ye are washed, but ye are sanctified, but ye are justified in the name of the Lord Jesus, and by the Spirit of our God" (1 Cor. 6:11).

Given this scoop for fending off the bullying tactics of doubt, going forward it is crucial to keep your ears open and tuned-in with the Word of God. When the bell rings again and the gloves come off, the only thing your opponent—doubt—will see are clean hands. There is more. Not only are your hands clean, but you are sealed by the Holy Ghost unto the day of redemption. I was sealed at a Tuesday Night Prayer Meeting at Bailey Cathedral Church of God in Christ. I was seeking the baptism of the Holy Ghost. They told me to keep saying "Thank You Jesus" which I did. I kept at it, saying "Thank you Jesus" until eventually my tongue got away from me and I was filled with the Holy Ghost! Have you not heard? God gives us the Holy Ghost as a down payment on our ultimate and complete glorification in heaven, "that being the earnest of our inheritance until the redemption of the purchased possession, unto the praise of his glory" (Ephesians 1:14).

With this kind of future ahead, do you really care about the confrontations of your past? Doubt has no place in your future, so do not give it any room in your present, much less your future. Doubt knows exactly how to throw you off track with the most vivid, cunning and crafty distractions. And just for kicks, at just the right moment, doubt will expose its obnoxious tendencies by provoking you to act out of character. Then, once you begin acting out of character, you will only have to work twice as hard to reel yourself back into your rightful role, conduct and demeanor as a member of Christ's chosen generation, "those who are sanctified in Christ Jesus, called to be saints, with all who in every place call upon the name of Jesus Christ our Lord, both theirs and ours" (1 Cor. 1:2).

Rather than act out of character, Habakkuk fully intends to stand at his watch to hear what the Lord will say. Meanwhile, do you remember God's command through the mouth of Moses to the ears of the people? "Fear ye not. Stand still and see the salvation of the Lord." Do not be deceived however: standing still does not mean running with the multitude or mingling with everybody everywhere. Standing still demands an attitude of sanctification—separation—so that you can maintain a holy posture at a time when you desperately need to hear from a holy God. It turns out that Habakkuk's waiting was time well spent. He was not disappointed. The Lord ordered that he write the vision which would come to him so the people could read it. At the same time, he was reminded that its fulfillment would come in God's good time. Sadly, and far too often, we yearn for God to answer, move and expedite His work in our time—typically quick, fast and in a hurry. But because our God sees the past, present and future all at the same time, He has a different outlook, His own timetable, for everything. His view is quite different from ours, because while we can easily become behaviorally cramped by our own limitations of what we see, God's knowledge is unlimited. We can only see what is, but God can see what was, what is and what will be all at that same time.

God sees your past. He knows exactly what happened: Babies born to unwed teens. College students dropped out. Young adults from working families at every socio-economic level stumbled into chemical dependencies by experimenting with alcohol and a limitless supply of recreational narcotics. The temptation to steal became overpowering. Pistols were fired. When questioned, your parents were told lies. It happened. Being in the wrong place at the wrong time happened, and whether you were an accomplice or not, you easily became an innocently bystanding victim of someone else's chronic wrongdoing. It happened. One thing led to another. Juvenile curiosity led to promiscuity. Promiscuity led to mind games. Mind games led to street hustling. Street hustling spilled over into swindling; swindling led to a shakedown; the shakedown led to incarceration. It happened. Terminated from a job because of a foolish mistake. Silenced by your home Church because a moment of temptation overtook you. We have all somehow been touched by these regrettable episodes of bad judgement. Yet all of our stories are different: You may look back over the years and shake your head in disbelief over how you were able to become carried away with folly, constantly needing approval from the wrong people; allowing yourself to become caught up in dangerous, even criminal, juvenile antics; ignoring the screeching loud, red flags flashing in your face; displaying outright disobedience to authority; looking the other way to the mistreatment of others; abandoning the values by which you were raised; foolishly placing your life—and the lives of others—in harm's way; poorly managing your vulnerabilities; caving-in to your weaknesses; creating distressing circumstances for people who love you, all because you failed to keep your word; prioritizing your flesh over your faith; blindly diving into danger; never taking a single moment to consider the consequences—and all along the way, lying to cover your tracks. Yes, we have all been there!

While everyone has their own story, there lies beneath all of these episodes of carelessness, a loose thread. Once this loose thread is pulled, it causes your entire family, your friends and loved ones to become completely unraveled. Just ask Habakkuk. He is in real pain watching his own people seemingly go down with a nation of reckless transgressors, idolaters—worshippers of the sun-god, the moon-god, the city-god, the thunder-god and so on and on. He is helpless. What about today? Are there no hands to pull us out of the fire when faced with these realities? Yes, there are. Eventually, help indeed arrives on the horizon. Rescue happens. Rehabilitation happens. God has intentionally equipped the mind of man to conceive and skillfully execute reliable systems of clinical treatment. It is always a ray of hope. It is refreshing! Broken pieces are mended. Family breaches are repaired. Fractured relationships are restored. Tensions around the dinner table are relaxed. You can breathe easily. Things start looking better.

Then periodically, comes the relapse. It happens unfortunately. Not always, but from time to time. An objective voice, speaking from personal experience describes, "Relapse is a sense of failure. Relapse means this kind of concept of falling right back into it, back where you were. When what's really happening is that I'm moving on all the time; sometimes it's two steps forward one step back, but I'm always learning and moving on. Relapse means going right back to the start and nobody can stand to think like that." This is all too real. No need for shame, however. You are not alone. None of this takes God by surprise. Search the Scriptures—The entire cycle of the Judges of Israel was depicted by one relapse after another.

After the death of Moses and his successor Joshua, the time came in those days when there was no king in Israel and "every man did that which was right in his own eyes" (Judges 21:24-25).

Only sporadically was there peace in the land.

Then the cycle:

1. Israel served the Lord.
2. Israel then did evil in the eyes of the Lord.
3. God punished Israel. They were enslaved.
4. Israel cried out unto the Lord.
5. God raised up a judge.
6. Israel was delivered.
7. There was peace in the land again.
8. Israel served the Lord again.
9. Relapse: Israel did evil in the eyes of the Lord.

All throughout the book of Judges, the cycle repeats itself over and over.

Do not ever doubt, downplay or second-guess the power working within you to pull down those strongholds. You have been already given the authority to rebuke the shame of relapses. Say it out loud, "I rebuke the shame of relapses!" You are no less important than the person who has never relapsed—still God's creation, still "fearfully and wonderfully made" to make God's praises glorious in all the earth! So, you can tell doubt to go somewhere and mind its own business.

Stay alert! Between each cycle of our personal relapses, doubt will always seize the opportunity to plant the seed of hopelessness. This seed cannot flourish however. Anything that springs up is doomed to be quickly cut down like the grass. It is doomed to be wiped out by the sharp, swift, decisive and sanctified "washing of water by the Word" (Ephesians 5:26).

This washing by the Word blots out all those immature decisions made during those painful years of developing into a responsible adult. The Word of God furnishes the calm assurance that these brick walls are not necessarily dead ends: "Though he fall, he is not utterly cast down" (Psalms 37:24). Do you believe this?

Then you can now take the first step towards your future by envisioning yourself an overcomer! You have no other choice. Even clinical rehabilitation and counseling is ill-fated if approached while flirting with doubt. While you are at it, envision yourself a fully recovered trooper in the Lord's army. Envision yourself getting back up again, and again, and again. Your successful recovery has only as much backbone as your faith in the yoke-breaking deliverance from the healing hands of your Lord and Savior Jesus Christ. This requires remaining steadfast, totally delinquent of any doubt throughout the entire course of treatment—relapses and all. For whom the Son makes free—without a doubt—is "free indeed" (John 8:36).

Next, **God sees your present**. He knows precisely where you are. He is divinely tapped into your current circumstances—good days and so-called bad days—are ever before Him. Smiles and tears. Heartaches and happiness. Who knows? Perhaps building trust has been an issue in the past with disappointing results. Do not fret. Never doubt that you can completely trust God. With total confidence that His eyes are upon your predicament, go ahead and let God, Who loves you, heal you. Like no one else, He cares about the burden you carry and the bleeding struggle which aggravates every grain of your patience. If you would only give-in to Him, He will freely exercise His loving power over you as the potter does the clay. He will fully develop, perfect and polish you—again, only if you let Him. All of those imperfections caused by the bruises of your past are already worked into His plan for completing the magnificent work of the all-unique you! Be vigilant. Stay sober. Clear your head. Make certain you do not become the browbeater who holds *yourself* back. To that point, I consistently advise young people, "Be careful what you do now. Don't let your present jeopardize your future."

Tread carefully and prayerfully. Do not become stranded upstream, baffled by waves from your past. You are not a loser. This is not your story. You have heard the Word, your heart has been touched, your spirit has been pricked by the Holy Ghost and you have happily tasted the heavenly gift. Give away no ground. Confess that you are unwilling to turn back, no matter how frequently doubt may pick a fight with you by bringing up a bad day, aggravated by a bad decision, during a bad period in your past. You are so much better than that! And doubt, along with its nasty little imps, knows it as well. I contend to those who don't consider themselves young anymore, do not let your past hold you hostage. But so far, thanks to your willingness to "trust in the Lord with all your heart," doubt is making a mockery of itself and clearly facing a losing battle.

Finally, **God sees your future**. Your future has already been ordered to unfold in the peace and joy of His eternal presence. This is an everlasting hope demonstrated by every new sunrise. God's daily keeping power is broadcast by Jude, "Now unto him that is able to keep you from falling, and to present you faultless before the presence of his glory with exceeding joy."

From sunrise to sunset, Habakkuk waited. But he did not wait idly. He waited faithfully. There is no other way to expect the kind of results which will directly benefit your spiritual development. While your trial is in session, your faithful wait is actively stimulating the work of patience within you. Got it? Good. Because not only does faith stimulate patience, but patience, experience; and experience, hope: And hope maketh not ashamed; because the love of God is shed abroad in our hearts by the Holy Ghost which is given unto us" (Romans 5:4-5). There is no reason, therefore, to allow doubt to make you feel inferior to warriors like Habakkuk. Though he was a professional prophet, he too had to grow into his place of patience. Though he eventually made the mature decision to wait on God, it was not quite the decision he necessarily would have made just a few verses earlier. He had to grow into it. In a nutshell, our growing process boils down to two realities: *time* and *preparation*. I hope you hear me–it's a process! If I may take it a step further: plenty of folk want to shine, but no one wants to be polished! They want to play in the game, but they don't want to show up for practice.

I am no cook, but Karen is a tremendous cook. She remains diligent even with her busy schedule. One of the most exciting times for me is during the holidays. It happens on a regular basis when we are anticipating this great meal. Of course, for whatever reasons, our families are never on time for dinner. So, you go through the whole day anticipating this great feast at 3:30 PM, but it never happens. You try not to mess up your appetite and what happens is that dinner ends up being served at about 5:30 PM. Of course, by this time, you have waited so long until you cannot eat that much, and you feel cheated. It never fails though—The longer the wait, the stronger the simmering of spices, juices, seasonings and flavor. The meal prep time always turns out to be well worth the scrumptious feast ultimately.

In God's eyes, *preparation time* is *precious time.* To be sure, "the trial of your faith (being much more precious than gold that perisheth, though it be tested with fire) might be found unto praise and honor and glory at the appearing of Jesus Christ" (1 Peter 1:7).

For now, perhaps all you can see is yourself in that desperate situation. But God, in His divine foreknowledge is far ahead of you. He sees you coming out of your situation unharmed. At the same time, He is controlling the speed limit like only a loving Father can. Fact: God will always honor your faith by taking you higher. However, if you go up too fast, you will come down too hard. And the only way to get up, dust yourself off and stand on your own two feet is by completely turning your back on doubt and turning up your faith. Put it on blast that God will bring you into what He promised!

From Habakkuk to the Apostle Paul, no one claims to have it all figured out. Paul flatly admits, "I count not myself to have apprehended: but this one thing I do, forgetting those things which are behind, and reaching forth unto those things which are before, I press toward the mark for the prize of the high calling of God in Christ Jesus" (Philippians 3:13-14).

All of us have a past, but your past need not have you. We have all had to experience the growing pains of getting to where God has ordained for us to be. When I first began to pastor at Greater Emmanuel, the congregation only consisted of eight parishioners. It was okay. Actually, I found the challenge very exciting! I was young, eager, ready to build, expand and grow.

And so I went straight to work: Preaching, winning souls, posting billboards, spreading the Word, inviting anybody and everybody to Christ. The people began to come. They were hungry for God. They were walking into the Church with all kinds of wounds, often beat down by all kinds of devastating experiences and hardships. Still, they were showing up! One weekend, a sister showed up whose appearance instantly reminded me of a carhop from the 60s: Shapely, with slim-fitting jeans and a sweatshirt. She asked, "Pastor, is it alright if I wear what I have on?" Doing my best, as always, to be warm, welcoming and inclusive, I graciously replied, "Of course, you can!" She then proceeded to lift up her sweatshirt to show me her customized t-shirt creatively designed with a somewhat undignified street phrase spelled-out with a four-letter cuss word emblazoned across the front. In a flash, I had to pull back my words, "Oh no, dear!"

That was a close call (to say the least). Not to even mention the nearby occasion when another sister from the neighborhood showed up for worship wearing short jeans–very short jeans– and a halter top. (Lord, have mercy!) She didn't know any better. So sincere. So innocent. So harmless. However, apparently at some point during the worship service, one of the Church Mothers approached her, removed her shawl, wrapped it around the young lady (keep in mind, nobody knows this young lady) and scolded her, "Don't you ever come up in here looking like that!"

Whenever souls are at stake, there is no time to waste. I had to deal with this at once, with no choice except to call the Mother into my office (which at the time was no more than a room with barely enough space, at my height, to stand up and sit back down, much less turn around).

I calmly got to the point,

"Mother, I was informed of what happened today. It seems you were kind of rough on the young lady, don't you think?"

Mother fired right back,
"Yea, she looked a mess! This ain't no club!"

I leaned forward and lovingly expressed,

"Mother, I appreciate what you're doing to help me build the Church, but you can't clean the fish until you catch them!"

If doubt had its way, I would have dismissed the young lady at first sight, never looking past her outward appearance, never appreciating the purity of her heart, never giving her a chance to enter into a personal relationship with Jesus Christ where she could be taught, seasoned, nurtured and begin to grow. Again, all of us have a past, but your past need not have you.

Right now all eyes are on you. Your reactions will determine the narrative of this moment. Do not slip into complacency. Crank up your faith, get over that bridge and get ready for a whole new world to open up before your very eyes. Once you get into position and make up your mind to see the salvation of the Lord, you will discover the seriousness of treating yourself better. Taking a brutal beating over poor choices of the past is one of the most all-too-common types of self- abuse. At the same time, it is meaningless. It is as brutal as it is pointless. You cannot change your past anymore than you can manipulate yesterday's mercies to accommodate today's challenges. This is why God has freely given you brand new mercies, layered upon His unfailing compassion, renewed morning by morning, infused with His faithfulness. What a package! Renewed mercies, unfailing compassion, inexhaustible faithfulness–all in the same breath!

It gets even better. Listen carefully: "For while we were still weak, at the right time Christ died for the ungodly. For one will scarcely die for a righteous person–though perhaps for a good person one would dare even to die but God shows his love for us in that while we were still sinners, Christ died for us. Since, therefore, we have now been justified by his blood, much more shall we be saved by him from the wrath of God. For if while we were enemies we were reconciled to God by the death of his Son, much more, now that we are reconciled, shall we be saved by his life. More than that, we also rejoice in God through our Lord Jesus Christ, through whom we have now received reconciliation" (Romans 5:6-11).

There is no room for doubt to wiggle its way into this kind of love. There is no room for doubt to stir up any further misunderstanding over your pure intentions. Actually, if doubt had its way, your good, kind and giving heart would stay broken indefinitely. Every time doubt takes a swipe at you, it is aimed at crushing your heart. But you and I both know you have another brilliant move tucked away. It involves a lightening-fast countermove to a jab. Here is how it maneuvers: The rear shoulder is lunged forward while the dominant hand is held back, snug against your face. Your upper and lower body dance across the ring counterclockwise as the punch is thrown into the face of doubt. The name of the move—The Cross. Quick recap: Watch out for those devious reminders of your past. Get ready to dance across the ring counterclockwise. Keep your mind fixed on the Cross. Stay focused on the real issues. You are no longer bouncing around the ring with unsettled issues. Your mind is on the Cross because that is where those past issues were put to rest forever. After all, while Christ was on the Cross, guess who was on His mind. You were! One more time: Watch out for those trifling little hints from your past. Don't let anything break your spirit. Keep your mind on the Cross and get ready to dance! Hang in there! Listen carefully, you and I have every reason in the world to trust God. Let me tell you about the God I serve: The God I serve keeps His promise. With that promise, you can walk on through your storm and watch God come through for you—every time. In fact, if I were you, I wouldn't wait until this bout is over, I would praise Him right now!

Despite how arrogantly your past may try to capture and hold you hostage, I need you to know that your future is brighter than ever and worth the battle. Please hear me, when you step into that ring, strapped tight with your faith, God will come through for you. The same God Who touches sick bodies, Who heals wounded hearts–He will come through for you! He may seem silent at times, but He is always working. Here's what you need to know: God is stronger than any opponent. Whatever is going on, never let anything or anyone break your spirit. God is still in control. So, keep on walking by faith. No matter what you are going through, God is going to bring you out. Stand back and don't be surprised. Because when God gets ready, He is going to do His thing. And when His thing is done, doubt is defeated! When His thing is done, and the votes are counted, you win! I have a clear memory in my mind, while in the Fourth Grade, being nominated captain of the baseball team. The teacher made us, the nominees, put our faces to the wall while the rest of the team voted. Turns out I ended up losing by only one vote. When I returned home and told my mother what had happened, she lovingly reproved me, "Oh no baby, you *always* vote for yourself!" And I've been doing just that ever since. Lesson learned. Never forgotten.

Time check: Round Two is about to begin. Once again, everyone settle into place. No walking. Are you ready to make your move? Are you prepared to hold on faithfully with Habakkuk? Are you ready to step into the ring and pull out that cross punch? Are you ready to wait, watch and dance? Are you ready to practice being brand new? By the way, this goes for you and any other man or woman who is in Christ Jesus. You are a new creature! Old things are passed away. Behold, all things are new! (2 Cor. 5:17). This applies even when you do not feel brand new! And, on those days when you do not feel new, do not let doubt carry you back to those things which are old.

If you know for sure you are ready, from here on out, there is no longer any such attitude as "win, lose or draw." It is always a win. And you are the winner, because this time around, you're going to vote for yourself!

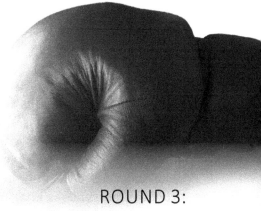

A BOUT WITH THE CHALDEANS (PEOPLE)

T hey are powerful. They are shrewd. They are dominant and forceful. They are united. Who are we talking about? The Chaldeans. Without question, each of us has our own group of Chaldeans—large or small—to deal with on an ongoing basis. In all fairness, ample warning was given to Habakkuk: "For behold, I am raising up the Chaldeans, that bitter and hasty nation, who march through the breadth of the earth, to seize dwellings not their own" (Habakkuk 1:6).

These are the dream-snatchers. These are the groups whom we can always count on to put us down at that very moment when we have mustered up the energy to pull ourselves up! These are the co-workers, neighbors, acquaintances, teammates, classmates, play cousins and family members who always know how to say exactly the wrong thing. These are the voices that place a strain on our inner peace. These are the familiar circles of people whose dialogue is about as useful as food poisoning. These are the people who take deep dives into doubt and are forever looking for diving partners. Their *modus operandi* flaunts the notion, if you cannot beat them, join them. Too often, if you cannot beat them, they will beat you with their harsh insensitive words until you crack under pressure and go along with their heathen ways.

Doubt begets misery and misery loves company. Misery therefore seeks out to exert its influence through the social strain of voices, behaviors, habits, trends and crazes. Especially in this generation, unscrupulous social influence has become a force of enormous proportions—untamed, unchecked and underestimated. The American Psychological Association defines social influence as "any change in an individual's thoughts, feelings, or behaviors caused by other people, who may be actually present or whose presence is imagined." Write this down if you must. This will be our principal focus.

By and large, these social influences are delivered through the power of words—and words have power! All it takes is one word of encouragement to give your dream the boost it needs. Conversely, it only takes one word of discouragement to puncture your confidence and hitch up a partnership with doubt. What a pair! Discouragement and doubt. Barely a stone's throw from bitterness. Discouragement and doubt will shut you down and shut you out. They will talk you into neglecting your gift. They will egg on the impulse to withdraw your reasonable service. They will invite you to mixers where discouragement, doubt and bitterness have matured, where they roll out the amenities of despondency until your perspective is blindsided by an automated agenda of whining and complaining. It all starts with a word. Typically, a wrong word at the wrong time from the wrong person who carries the wrong sphere of influence.

Doubt is a tiny seed, barely visible. But like any seed, for doubt to germinate, it must first be planted. Given just the right downpour of rainfall, it eventually branches out, bearing buds of influence. As revealed in Scripture, some are obviously more easily influenced than others. The fact remains, whenever doubt speaks loud enough, and we are easily persuaded by what we hear, influence is not far behind shifting into gear. Putting your foot down and resisting the pull of social influences is always easier said than done. Later on, when we arrive at Mount Carmel, we will see how standing alone, outnumbered by idol-worshipping heathens, is not only possible, but pleasing before God.

So, what exactly does it take for us to be lured into the behavior of others—good or bad? First, experience teaches that you cannot casually entertain doubt. You cannot invite doubt to take a seat on your front porch, gussied up with lemonade and shortbread. You cannot welcome doubt into the sanctity of your living room to make its pitch and sell you a lie craftily designed to turn you away from your faith in the true and living God. But it happens.

The power of persuasion begins early and follows you as far as you are willing to be followed and harassed. Some 30 miles away from our home, in Flint Michigan, five teenagers concocted a fatal so-called "prank" of rock-throwing from a highway overpass. The prank was known as "pinging", resulting in the death of a highway passenger: a husband, a father, a son. Upon their arrest, each teen's level of participation was revealed, begging the question: How does this mindset of delinquent conduct gain a following? At what point does this conduct seem like a good idea? The American Academy of Child and Adolescent Psychiatry suggests that pre- adolescents simply do not possess the skills to think clearly, rationally or responsibly enough to weigh the consequences of such a grossly outrageous "prank". They simply lack the discipline.

The discipline to sanctify ourselves from outside influences was the principle behind God's injunction against idolatry. God wants your worship, singularly and exclusively. Yet the connection between expressing worship and exterminating doubt is not an insignificant one. Once you have been a direct partaker of the goodness of the Lord, no one has to influence your passion for worship. There remains a critical reality: Cults, conspiracies, creeds, cliques and crowds have arrested and assaulted the minds of God's people since—and long before—the years of Habakkuk's prophetic career. At its root, the common denominator: Doubt. When God handed down the Law to Moses, he directed Moses to command the Children of Israel to bring up their children in the way, to write the Law upon the tables of their hearts, with the promise that it would keep them and be well with them. Right off the top was the foremost command: "Thou shalt have no other gods before me." God was making it as plain as the rainbow in the sky when the flood waters receded that He was absolutely not going to tolerate His worship being ascribed to any other. No questions. No discussion. No exceptions. Still there is a subtle transaction that takes place whenever the voice of skepticism flirts with our faith. God does not reveal Himself through skepticism, but God has revealed Himself through His Word. This revelation positions us to adopt the mindset that to know God is to first know His Word. Along your journey, as knowledge increases, so must your zeal for searching Him out. In fact, God says, "You'll find me when search for me with your whole heart" (Jeremiah 29:13).

Habakkuk already knows God. He knows Who God is. He has yet to discover Who God is *not*. Steadily, he is on the path to discover that God is not a man that He should lie. He is also set in place upon his watchtower to discover that God's thoughts are not our thoughts, neither are His ways our ways, especially when surrounded by the influences of the wicked. At some point in our journey, we will be confronted with a lie cleverly disguised as truth. The disguise will be accompanied by a voice which sounds credible, sensible and quite believable. This is why it is so important to stay on high alert: No question about it, the devil is a liar. However, many people say the devil tells *only lies*. But I disagree. How could Eve be influenced by Satan if he only told lies? My contention is that the devil does not tell *only lies*. Often he tells the truth to lure us into believing the big lie—the belief that he *really isn't* who he *really is*. His technique is spelled out in Genesis 3:1 when he said unto the woman, "Yea, hath God said, 'Ye shall not eat of every tree of the garden'?" He replays himself in Matthew 4:6 while reciting the Word of God to Jesus Himself in the wilderness, "and said unto him, If thou art the Son of God, cast thyself down, for it is written, He shall give his angels charge concerning thee, and in their hands they shall bear thee up lest at any time thou dash thy foot against a stone." Just think, if the devil only told lies, it would be a cinch for us to resist him. His craft is to manipulate our actions by stumping us with the truth.

For the time being, the task before you is to peel back that disguise and recognize it for what it is: Who planted that insidious morsel of doubt in your spirit? Who introduced you to the behavior of questioning the validity of what God proposed to accomplish when He saved you? Who sabotaged your self-esteem? Who came along and told you what you could not do after you had already dared to dream that you could? Whom did you allow to shove you aside, take the wheel and assume control over your self-worth as a legitimate child of God? Who planted in your head the notion that there are multiple ways to God, other than through Jesus Christ—and that you can act up now and repent later? Who floated the suggestion that you could gain the world without risking your soul? Whose words made you numb to the consequences of your actions? Who in the world belittled the power of your common sense? Getting to the bottom of that influential party was a priority for Malcolm X. He was all too eager to find the culprits among his people: "Who taught you to hate the color of your skin? Who taught you to hate the texture of your hair? Who taught you to hate the shape of your nose and the shape of your lips? Who taught you to hate yourself from the top of your head to soles of your feet?"

Who is that one culpable instigator? How did their words push you over the top, past your willingness to fight back? Worse still, was it so bad that you were actually prepared to buckle under the social pressure and deny the fundamental tenets of your faith? For some of us, it was a close call! It was so close a call that we have learned to subconsciously block out of our minds the fact that someone's words nearly once crushed us to pieces. Listen up! Whomever they were, whomever they are—forgive them, for they know not what they do. Also, because they obviously never received the memo that "life and death are in the power of the tongue" (Proverbs 18:21). At the same time, hold your ground and remain assertive without being aggressive. What's the difference? Assertiveness involves respect for yourself and the person who offended you. Aggressiveness, on the other hand, can become quickly unglued leading to lashing out, disrespect and often insults. No one benefits from that, especially since you will only walk away feeling guilty or angry over words you cannot take back.

Instead, consider the lingering question: How did we come to this point where nothing seems sacred anymore? When did we decide that anything goes? When did we get to the place where we say whatever we want, do whatever we want, to whomever we want, no fear of God, no consideration for how hard it hits nor how severely it paralyzes the passion to soar higher in God? How do we rationalize these decisions?

According to *Psychology Today*, "There are two types of rationalization that people commonly engage in: prospective and retrospective. Prospective rationalizing refers to rationalizing a decision before making it, whereas retrospective rationalizing refers to rationalizing a decision after the fact." Their research goes on to say, "The field of behavioral economics demonstrated that people are not always rational when it comes to decision making." To add broader context, Karyn Hall, PhD provides in her article *What is Validation and Why Do I Need to Know?* "Validation is a simple concept to understand but difficult to put into practice. Validation is the recognition and acceptance of another person's internal experience as being valid. Emotional validation is distinguished from emotional invalidation, in which your own or another person's emotional experiences are rejected, ignored, or judged. Self-validation is the recognition and acknowledgement of your own internal experience." Sadly, we find ourselves often eager to accept validation from the worst possible influences which, when coping with the sting of personal disappointment, is better than no acceptance at all. This reveals how easily we can become uprooted and carried away. We are vulnerable. In our vulnerability, we are wide open to attack.

David, to his credit, exercised extreme self-control when he was faced with an invasion from the South by the Amalekites, typical to Habakkuk's scenario. They had taken the women captive and carried them away (1 Samuel 30:1-2). Then came that one word which would drive a hole through David's heart. That word came from the people. The people "spake of stoning him." They were disappointed in him. That had to hurt! Notice the immediate impact: "David was greatly distressed." Matters could not have been worse, "because the soul of all the people was grieved, every man for his sons and for his daughters." But his distress was counteracted when he pulled himself together and "encouraged himself in the Lord his God" (1 Samuel 30:6).

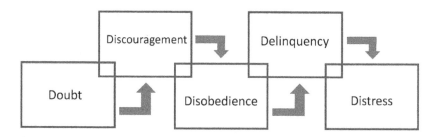

Therefore, consider this: The Chaldeans, as powerful, shrewd, dominant and forceful as they may be, are just people! They are ordinary, fallible people created by the same God Who created you fearfully and wonderfully, crowning you with a free will. Surely, just as the Spirit of God moved upon the face of the waters in Creation, nothing moves upon the free will of man with greater force or influence than the power of God's Word–no less assertively than He spoke light into existence in the beginning (Genesis 1:3).

Thinking back, all it took was one word for you to slip into a rut of discouragement wanting nothing more to do with anyone, much less working out your salvation with fear and trembling. Pinpoint the moment: It was only one word. But that one word alone cut through the delicate tissue of your self-esteem leaving you abandoned in a pool of pity, misery and hopelessness—dejected and distressed like Rachel who could not be consoled. You were ready like never before to cut your losses and walk away from everything and everybody.

Not so fast. Look up, straight ahead. This is not a dead end, it is merely a crossroad. Therefore, cutting your losses and walking away is not an option at this juncture. Just as it took only one word to place you in this stupor, your complete deliverance from this state of discombobulation is hinged upon the power of just one word. Sidebar: God's Word never runs empty! You do not need to look any further for validation, approval or acceptance from any more wrong places. You do not have to run with the crowd to be accepted. On the contrary, God has called you, never to fit in, but to stand out. It is high time that you take your rightful place in the royal priesthood again. One word started all of this and one word is going to put it to an end, once and for all!

First, let us identify the need. You do not need to be validated. You do not need to be affirmed. You do not need to be coddled. There is nothing wrong with your spiritual nervous system. There is nothing wrong with your senses. There is nothing wrong with your sense of taste; although nothing is palatable once bitterness sets in. There is nothing wrong with your sense of touch: You are still able to be touched by the hand of God, but you are reluctant to ask for it especially since the last time you needed to be touched, instead you ended up hurt—and very badly. There is nothing wrong with your sense of smell: You have not become so desensitized that you do not long for the aroma of the anointing that once rested upon your countenance whenever you submerged yourself in the rapture of prayer.

One more diagnostic test. You may possibly have a few mild symptoms of poor eyesight. But do not panic. It is a known fact, according to Mary Bates' article, *Super Powers for the Blind and Deaf,* "if one sense is lost, the areas of the brain normally devoted to handling that sensory information do not go unused—they get rewired and put to work processing other senses." Popularly known as the Ray Charles Effect, poor eyesight allows for razor-sharp, crystal-clear hearing! Researchers agree, "a young child who is blind develops a keen ability to hear things that others cannot." And vice-versa? Well, Melissa Malzkuhn, who conducts presentations for first-year students at Gallaudet University's Visual Language and Visual Learning Center says, "I ask them if they think that deaf people see better. And oftentimes the students say, 'Yes!' Malzkuhn, who is deaf, says through an interpreter. "And so I tell them that science actually says that we don't see better. We just see differently. Which is an eye-opening experience to them."

Habakkuk, on his watchtower, knows full well what he is seeing. Though at the moment, he is not seeing clearly. His vision is somewhat blurred. Things are not always as they seem. His perspective is slightly out of focus. If you recall, no diagnosis of poor eyesight—natural or spiritual– was too complicated for our Savior. After He had interrupted the noise carried on by the professional mourners at the ruler's house, after He had raised his young daughter who was perceived dead (by those who had poor spiritual eyesight), two blind men followed Him, crying out, "Thou son of David, have mercy on us." When they went so far as to follow Jesus into the house, it was a dead giveaway–they clearly were craving an intervention! Christ went ahead and asked them, point blank, "Believe ye that I am able to do this?" Great question.

Do you believe God is able to do this? Habakkuk? Do you believe God is able to tear down the empire of the Chaldeans? According to Daniel's interpretation of Nebuchadnezzar's dream, it is only a matter of time anyway. Do you believe God is able to rescue His beloved people from captivity? Do you believe He is able to set you free and bring you back home? The question is firm: "Do you believe I am able to do this or not?" Yes or no.

When confronted with the life-changing question, "Do you believe I am able to do this?" the blind men had only one reply: They said unto him, Yea, Lord. There it is–loud and clear! The classic cry of the true believer, "Yes Lord!" When you find yourself at the end of your rope and the end of the rope is unraveling, and crumbling to pieces—call up, awaken, stir up the power of the "Yes, Lord!" Your "Yes, Lord" covers a lot of emotional territory. It solidifies your rank as a die-hard believer. It cannot be overstated—The power of your personal confession, "Yes, Lord" is alive and well. It has never ceased to render sweet music before the Lord. "Yes, Lord!" Not a manufactured "Yes Lord!" but a submissive "Yes, Lord!" You must say it like you mean it and mean it like you say it, "Yes, Lord!"

Jesus's "Yes, Lord" in the Garden of Gethsemane the night before He was arrested cleared the runway for our salvation (Matthew 26:39). It is therefore irreversible and beyond recall. If somehow you have misplaced your "Yes, Lord!" go find it! It will sharpen your hearing and restore your visibility all at once. No need in obeying the command to take up your bed and walk if you cannot first see yourself ever walking again. You must believe! If you cannot see yourself healed, why bother calling for the elders of the Church? (James 5:14). Frankly, if you don't see it before you see it, you will *never* see it. When Jesus touched the eyes of the two blind men saying, "according to your faith be it unto you" their eyes were opened. But not before they gave Him a firm, passionate, up-front "Yes, Lord!" (Matthew 9:29-30).

Once you have confessed your sincere "Yes Lord," do not become complacent. Instead, get ready and get out of the way for God to take over. Sometimes God has to take you through something to get you to your destination. My destination, per the orchestration of the Holy Ghost, was my beloved Greater Emmanuel Church embedded in the heart of Highland Park, surrounded by Detroit. But God had to take me through something. It all came about when I accepted an invitation to speak at Greater Emmanuel for Resurrection Morning Worship 1988. My level of excitement and eagerness to stand before this congregation and deliver God's Word was no small matter, seeing that the Church was without a pastor, and I was being seriously considered. Very humbling. Back at my desk, I was completely engrossed in the task of completing my Master's Thesis; so engrossed that the time got away from me–*literally got away*. By the time I placed the finishing touches on my compelling dissertation on fractions–of all mathematical problems, fractions–I was now ready to preach! My sermon was ready. The Word which the Holy Spirit dropped in my heart to share was alive, "quick and powerful." Nothing could slow me down nor hold me back from making my way to this waiting house, to these precious saints who were without a shepherd. Imagine my bewilderment when I arrived, walked through the doors of that sanctuary only to discover the worship service was already an hour in progress. My obvious reaction, "What's going on?" It turns out, that specific day, Resurrection Sunday, April 3, 1988, fell on the same day which commenced Daylight Savings Time. Would you believe, with all my excitement, my readiness, my enthusiasm (and all of my fractions), I had not bothered to re-set my clock an hour ahead? Doubt immediately lit into my ear, "There's no way you're going to get to Pastor this Church!" But it was okay. No need to fret. No need to sweat it. God had already established this time and season for my life in the secret chambers of His holiness. The Word came forth. The Spirit of God moved mightily. The house was blessed. Souls came to Christ. Lives were changed and the rest is history. Precisely one week after graduating Wayne State University with my Master's of Education in Mathematics, I began pastoring Greater Emmanuel Church of God in Christ. What a mighty God we serve! No doubt about it, when God is ready to open doors, He sets the hour Himself and it is fixed. Fixed—not like an amateur prize fight—but fixed with destiny. Fixed by the holy hands of a mighty God Who had already begun a good work and had already made my heart ready for Him to perform it, polish it and perfect it unto the day of Jesus Christ. I'm a front row witness, God's providence defies explanation! On several occasions, I was offered Churches with far more members. Over and again, I was asked by my peers, "With your level of education and your background, why would you take that small church?" Because God's plan was in progress, and it was sealed with a promise. When I said "Yes" to the Lord, I was saying "Yes" to the journey, the press, the process and all that came along with it. Doubt had to die so that my destiny could live. Today, Greater Emmanuel is, by far, larger than all of the churches I was offered. God be praised! Even as a young boy, I knew Greater Emmanuel to have a rich history as a cornerstone house of worship in Highland Park. Who would ever have imagined I would one day assume Pastoral leadership of such a ministry fully committed to teaching, indoctrinating, empowering and guiding individuals—entire families—into a fulfilling relationship with Jesus Christ? God knew. My assignment was to only "Believe!"

Simple, transparent, and straightforward: "Believe". That one, single, unavoidable, constraining word is the total game changer: "Believe." Disbelief instigated by doubt got you into this slump. The power within you to "believe" will pull you out! Do not be deceived, it only takes one word: Believe. The evidence speaks for itself: "...these signs shall follow them that believe; In my name shall they cast out devils; they shall speak with new tongues; They shall take up serpents; and if they drink any deadly thing, it shall not hurt them; they shall lay hands on the sick, and they shall recover" (Mark 16:17-18).

A broken heart is no laughing matter. A wounded spirit is not as easily repairable when the blow is repeated. God sent His word to heal us, not to wound us. God gave us each other to build up one another in our most holy faith, not to tear one another down with negative ungodly Chaldean chatter. Enough is enough. Hence, you do not have to beat them, nor do you have to join them. Your duty is to resist them.

Follow-Up Steps and Aftercare Precautions

As followers of Christ, **stay under the radar as best you can**. This means quietly walking in love, "as Christ also hath loved us, and hath given himself for us an offering and a sacrifice to God for a sweet-smelling savour. But fornication, and all uncleanness, or covetousness, let it not be once named among you, as becometh saints; Neither filthiness, nor foolish talking, nor jesting, which are not convenient: but rather giving of thanks. For this ye know, that no whoremonger, nor unclean person, nor covetous man, who is an idolater, hath any inheritance in the kingdom of Christ and of God."

Carefully choose your company. There are some blessings you will enjoy because of who you hang around—and vice versa. Be watchful. As goes the old adage, "If you expect to fly high with eagles, you can't run with turkeys." Take inventory of your sur-roundings. Tap into the long- term advantage of your decision to allow specific individuals into your inner circle and everything that privilege has to offer. Yes, you will often have to fly solo, you will experience loneliness and there will be turbulence as you climb to your cruising altitude, but turbulence is the price you pay for flying high. As you conduct inventory, discern the motives of conversations around you. "Let no man deceive you with vain words: for because of these things cometh the wrath of God upon the children of disobedience. Be not ye therefore partakers with them. For ye were sometimes darkness, but now are ye light in the Lord: walk as children of light: (For the fruit of the Spirit is in all goodness and righteousness and truth;) Proving what is acceptable unto the Lord."

Outshine the lies you are told. Outgrow the discouragement you are thrown. "Have no fellowship with the unfruitful works of darkness, but rather reprove them. For it is a shame even to speak of those things which are done of them in secret. But all things that are reproved are made manifest by the light: for whatsoever doth make manifest is light. Wherefore he saith, Awake thou that sleepest, and arise from the dead, and Christ shall give thee light."

Avoid getting entangled in confusion. "See then that ye walk circumspectly, not as fools, but as wise, Redeeming the time, because the days are evil. Wherefore be ye not unwise, but understanding what the will of the Lord is. And be not drunk with wine, wherein is excess; but be filled with the Spirit; Speaking to yourselves in psalms and hymns and spiritual songs, singing and making melody in your heart to the Lord; Let no one's cruel words steal your joy. Rather, give thanks always for all things unto God and the Father in the name of our Lord Jesus Christ" (Ephesians 5:1-20).

Remember who you are. Remember what you believe. Nothing good can come from ever forgetting—much less doubting—what you already believe about the divine attributes of God, the quickening power of His Word, His commandments, His promises, the message of the Gospel, the story of redemption, the manifestation of miracles, the confession of sin, the proposition of personal salvation, the duty of repentance, the joy of being reconciled with God through Christ, the peace of God that surpasses understanding, the victory of deliverance, the consummate beauty of forgiveness, the exercise of sanctification, obedience, humility, holiness, the privilege of true worship, the free gift of grace and the wonderful, regenerating work of the Holy Ghost. In fact, do you remember what happened on that day, that great day during the feast of the Jews? Do you remember when Jesus stood up and cried out? Everyone heard Him, "If you believe on Me as the Scriptures have said, out of your belly shall flow rivers of living water!" (John 7:38).

David knew, as full well as Habakkuk, watching the prosperity of the wicked was both tough and tempting. The only thing tougher was his testimony of how he almost slipped up and ran with the wicked. But he quickly remembered the key: He had to believe. Having made a clean break from his doubt, he walked away believing with every fiber of his being to see the goodness of the Lord in the land of the living! (Psalm 27:13). He knew his worth. He knew his work. He knew his worship. He knew his purpose.

I thank God for making His purpose for my life clear from early on. I knew where I was headed and was not the least bit conflicted about how to get there. Ministry was not a probability; it was a priority. No question. No back and forth. No hesitation. No fluctuation. No bout. No doubt. My destination was fixed. Not just because I came up in a household where the Church was an extension of the home, and not just because I was raised in ministry, but because ministry was raised in me! There is a difference. Growing up, I was not just "around" the Church, but I was "in" the Church—and the Church was in me. There was absolutely no line of demarcation between my career goals and my spiritual goals. They were directly intertwined. Case in point: Upon graduating college, I initially wanted to become an accountant. It seemed like a lucrative career choice. I soon learned, however, that working for an accounting firm would likely consume a great deal of time, especially at the end of the month, reconciling accounts, crunching numbers and making sure everything balances. It would have involved a level of demand which would take me away from my duties as a minister. Scratch that. I then tossed around the idea of Social Work. Eventually, I arrived at the decision to become an educator. It was the perfect choice—A Math Teacher: Steady work, reliable income, nights free, weekends free and the summer months free. This would allow me to do what God had charged me to do! I was able to conduct revivals in the summer and not skip a beat in my career which would pick back up in the Fall. With the flame of Evangelism upon my lips, a burning passion in my heart for soul-winning, fastened to my faith, driven by God's direction for my life, my plans took shelter in His plans. My life purpose found its definition in the safest place in the whole wide world—in the will of God. (Thank you for that, Bishop Richard "Mr. Clean" White).

Unfortunately, not everyone is convinced of their true worth. It was a troubling night in 1835 for Charlotte Elliott, poet and editor, who struggled restlessly with the question of her self-worth. Her brother, Rev. H. V. Elliot, had planned a charity bazaar to provide scholarships to the daughters of local clergymen. But the night before the bazaar she tossed to and fro, troubled in her spirit by the distressing thoughts of feeling totally useless. It was not long before these thoughts gradually transitioned into an outright spiritual conflict. The next day, the busy day of the bazaar, "the troubles of the night came back upon her with such force" she felt they could be conquered only by the grace of God. And taking pen and paper from the table she deliberately set down in writing, for her own comfort, 'the formula' of her faith." Her trembling fingers gripped to the pen, gliding across the paper, she recited to herself the Gospel of pardon, peace, and heaven, gaining strength and encouragement from "the eternity of the Rock beneath her feet." Right then, right there, just as she was, she wrote the timeless hymn, the altar call sang during that great revival meeting in Charlotte, North Carolina in 1934, where Billy Graham, one of the world's greatest evangelists, first gave his life to the Lord:

Just as I am, without one plea,
But that Thy blood was shed for me,
And that Thou bidst me come to Thee,
O Lamb of God, I come, I come.

And if you, like Habakkuk, are torn and conflicted,

Just as I am, though toss'd about
With many a conflict, many a doubt,
Fightings and fears within, without,
O Lamb of God, I come, I come.

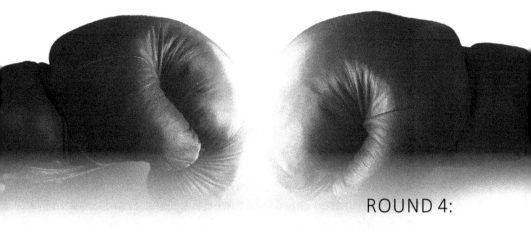

A BOUT WITH JUSTICE

O. J. Simpson, Casey Anthony, Scott Peterson and Derek Chauvin. We all know who they are. All four were handed indictments leading to what would become known as "Trials of the Century". All four stood their own trials tagged by overblown front-page news stories; back to back sensationalized media frenzy unheard of since the Lindbergh baby kidnapping. In each case, the moment eventually arrived for the trial judge to instruct the jury. On October 2, 1995, after eight months of testimony, the most notorious double-homicide of the century, *The People of the State of California v. Orenthal James Simpson*, was handed-off to a sequestered jury. The spotlight is on Lance Allan Ito, a University of California Berkley graduate, Presiding Judge over the infamous trial. He his firm. He is precise. He is straightforward: "You are reminded, that you must not be influenced by mere sentiment, sympathy, passion, prejudice, public opinion or public feeling. Both the prosecution and the defendant have a right to expect that you will conscientiously consider and weigh all of the evidence, apply the law as I have instructed you and reach a just verdict, regardless of the consequences." A heaping pile of over 1,000 pieces of evidence recorded upon 45,000 pages of trial transcript detailing the testimonies of more than 130 witnesses over the span of 267 days comprised the material they were entrusted to deliberate upon and arrive at a verdict: either an acquittal or a conviction "beyond a reasonable doubt."

The wait was on, but not for long. Barely four hours after Judge Ito's instructions, a verdict was reached. However, to add to the anxiety, Judge Ito took the extra step of triggering a worldwide epidemic of suspense by announcing that the verdict would not be read until the next morning at 10:00 AM. The wait was on again. By daybreak, a murky, dismal mood, daunted by saturated clouds scattered the skies. From coast to coast, the nation was on watch. Patrol was on high alert. Rodeo Drive in Beverly Hills was completely deserted. Morning rush hour traffic staggered with an awkward rhythm. From cafés to churches to board rooms to college dorms to suburban living rooms—restless agitation was in the air. Shoulder to shoulder, standing room only—the world watched. The palpitating heartbeat of anticipation could not be contained. The silence was deafening. Finally, the wait was over. Order in the court. Judge Ito enters and awaits the entry of the twelve jurors. Ten women, two men. They file into the courtroom, one by one and take their assigned seats in the jury box. No reactions, no subtle clues, no hints revealed on their complexions.

The defendant rises. The Court Clerk unseals the verdict. The cameras pan the courtroom audience. At that very moment, two families torn apart, seated opposite each other, share the agony of their nerves on total edge. The verdict is announced. The entire courtroom trembles. An earthquake would have been less staggering. High-pitched shrieks of disbelief are overheard in the streets. Tears of joy. Tears of anguish. A nation is divided. At the root of either side of the unmistakable reactions—glee and relief or shock and resentment—even until this day—remains one, lonely, pint-sized principle: reasonable doubt. This is the principle which slingshot every clear-thinking individual into their own worked-out conclusion of the trial: reasonable doubt. Word for word, "reasonable doubt" spells out "the legal burden of proof required to affirm a conviction in a criminal case. In a criminal case, the prosecution bears the burden of proving that the defendant is guilty beyond all reasonable doubt. This means that the prosecution must convince the jury that there is no other reasonable explanation that can come from the evidence presented at trial. In other words, the jury must be virtually certain of the defendant's guilt in order to render a guilty verdict."

As citizens of the kingdom, faced with our own trials, perplexed by our own trespasses, eyewitnesses to others, we are often too quick to exclaim what is "doubtful", likewise taking it upon ourselves to decide what is "reasonable." The lines are not always clear. Moreover, the question can be fashioned into many shapes and colors even as our Christian walk also takes shape. Where shall we begin? Is it reasonable that we are unable to determine the fulfillment of the Gospel we proclaim since we have no idea when Christ will return? Is it reasonable that earning the rank of a "good soldier" requires that we "endure hardness"? Some will doubt. While we are at it, how uneasy is it to swallow the fact that gifts are without repentance? Just how reasonable is it that the last shall be first and the first shall be last? Here and there, we keep swinging until we land a good hit. Sure, doubt knows how to swing back, but the swing is clumsy. You, on the other hand, are not as unskilled at drilling down on these questions as you think. You have more going for you than against you. You are quick on your feet, outfitted with the sharp, two-edge sword of the Word of God that cuts the dividing asunder of soul and spirit, "and of the joints and marrow, and is a discerner of the thoughts and intents of the heart" (Hebrews 4:12). The Word of God itself searches out what is intentional and premeditated; what is unintentional and impulsive; what is faultless and above suspicion. The Word of God, abiding within you, will always keep your faith in check, gaining traction with each test, forcing the silly, unsophisticated spirit of doubt back into a corner. Rude and uninvited, whenever doubt shows up to seduce us away from our faith, it is, by its very essence, unreasonable. Again, it turns up the noise of speculation fashioned as a long menu of questions: When a crime is committed, is it fair for the prosecution and defense to negotiate a plea agreement to reduce the penalty? Is it fair that the sentence imposed by Adam's crime was passed on to us, our children and their children? Is it then fair that we were born with a sinful nature? Is it really fair to be forced into reckoning with the idea that "He that believeth and is baptized shall be saved; but he that believeth not shall be damned"? By the same standard of fairness, how can we justify the plea agreement that was worked out and announced at Pentecost that "it shall come to pass that whosoever shall call upon the name of the Lord shall be saved?" More on that later. Still and all, the agreement appeals for the heart to believe unto righteousness with the mouth making confession unto salvation. Is it thus fair that the only way to God is through Jesus Christ, Him alone, and no other, despite our good works, charitable deeds, loving, compassionate, faithful and altruistic acts of humanity?

Basically, you cannot have it both ways. Either you accept God's nomenclature for justice accompanied by His plan for us to be saved, blood-washed and redeemed or you reject His execution of justice, making it impossible to receive His salvation and, in effect, toss out the baby with the bathwater. If it means getting up every single day, climbing into the ring and spending every waking hour fighting back with every ounce of strength— make up your mind!

You cannot go on wavering back and forth like a jittery, unstable wine bibber. You can no longer afford to make promiscuous advances at doubt by digging yourself into a rut, constantly asking questions for which you already know the answer: Is it fair and just that Job, an upstanding, respected citizen of Uz, should spend his life minding his own business, walking uprightly, eschewing evil and bothering nobody, only to become the target of Satan's attack—and with God's permission nonetheless? Is it fair and just that after God has boasted in Job's righteousness and corroborated his faithfulness, that his entire home should be stricken and fatally afflicted? Is it fair and just that his so-called friends should assign the blame to Job for his calamity—and get away with it? How could it be fair and just that the only choice Job is given on his bed of affliction is to either suffer until the end or curse God and die? Who could justify such an unreasonable, merciless ultimatum? (Job 2:9).

Furthermore, why must the wages of sin be death? Why such a harsh sentence? Why is there not a more equitable system in place to impose a lighter sentence upon first time offenders and a stiffer penalty upon repeat offenders? What exactly is the net gain of the rain falling equally on the just and the unjust? To clarify our Savior's point in Matthew 5:45, rain was extremely necessary and beneficial in Palestine. Likewise, the burning heat of the sun, particularly in Greece, usually signified God's power, while rain was an attribute of His benevolence. Yet God bestows it equally and unconditionally. What about the merit system? What is the purpose of allowing "bad things to happen to good people?" Violence, terminal illness, tragedy, hunger, domestic abuse– what is the point?

Faith McNulty's 1980 novel, *The Burning Bed*, portrays the violent physical abuse of Francine Hughes at the hands of her husband, James Berlin "Mickey" Hughes. The tragic events of her 13-year marriage came to a head on March 9, 1977 when Francine instructs her children to put their coats on and wait for her in the car parked outside their single-family home in Danville Michigan. She retrieves a gallon can of gasoline from the garage, tiptoes into the bedroom where her husband is drunk asleep, spews gasoline around the bed and ignites the flame. Instantly, the house goes up in blazes! With only seconds to spare, she rushes to her car where she cranks up and flees with her children in tow, straightaway to the local police precinct to confess her crime.

Alone, worn-down, indifferent and confused, Francine stands trial and is found to be not guilty by reason of temporary insanity. Analysts of the case point to the highly unusual decision of the defendant to testify at her own trial. Her passionate recount of the details of abuse by her husband won the sympathy of the jury, prompting their unanimous opinion that the murder was a justifiable action. Still many others strongly disagreed.

The plot unravels an irresistible sequence of events, carrying the reader inside both the wonderful world of law enforcement and the winding wilderness of the family court system while chipping away at the puzzling question: How could our system operate so carelessly to the point of practically blaming the victim for her own abuse—or at least whip up such a discriminatory notion? Kayleigh Roberts' article *The Psychology of Victim*

Blaming in The Atlantic, explains "When people want to believe that the world is just, and that bad things won't happen to them, empathy can suffer." She goes on to explain, "Any time someone defaults to questioning what a victim could have done differently to prevent a crime, he or she is participating, to some degree, in the culture of victim blaming." The National Domestic Violence Hotline points out, "The truth is that speaking out against abuse is not always a readily available option for people experiencing relationship abuse or sexual assault. We hear it from the thousands of people who reach out to The Hotline for help every day. We know that abuse thrives in isolation and that it walks hand-in-hand with fear. Fear muzzles the truth. It hides behind a veil of shame, and it rips you open from the inside out, making you feel like less of a person. We also know first-hand that fearing an abusive partner can be paralyzing, traumatizing, and have long-lasting effects on people's psyche and body. To understand violence, we need to accept that fear is a completely natural reaction to a threat, and therefore, it is OK to be afraid. What we can't do, however, is point fingers at the victims and blame them for not speaking out sooner. We are not in their shoes, and we will never know exactly how they feel."

In the case of Francine Hughes, she was driven to the point of despair by a defective law enforcement and family court system which left her helpless, hopeless and penniless. Her testimony upends the classic roller-coaster of reactions ranging from disbelief, despondency, bewilderment and shock to anger, rage and resentment. Whether shaking our head at Francine Hughes' "temporary insanity," Detective Mark Fuhrman perjuring himself on the witness stand, Casey Anthony's pathetic string of lies to the Orlando Police or the Chaldean Army surrounding Jerusalem, this well of emotions reveals our narrow understanding of fairness, justice, partiality and reasonableness executed by a holy God Who will bring into judgment both the righteous and the wicked. For there will be a time for every activity, a time to judge every deed (Ecclesiastes 3:17).

Fairness is purely subjective—influenced by our personal feelings. This includes our tastes and opinions. At the same time, the expression of such personal feelings is entirely human nature. Understandably then, Habakkuk is being only human in questioning, "Why is this happening and how is it just?" And off we go, back to the drawing board: Is it fair in any way that "the fathers have eaten sour grapes and their children's teeth are set on edge"? Straight out, God–conclusively and categorically–visits the sins of the fathers upon the children to the third and fourth generations. This arrangement of terms within the Law begs the nagging question overheard at after-hours get-togethers at Starbucks, chatter at the water cooler, the typical Monday Morning office banter, "How could a loving God send good people into suffering, punishment, judgement and damnation?" First things first: Who can manufacture the audacity to determine for themselves that they are, in the eyes of God, "good" or even righteous? By whose standards are these measurements taken? Who's setting the bar? How high (or low) is it being set? The answer quickly shows up in Scripture when Romans Chapter 3 quotes Psalm 14, "None is righteous, no, not one; no one understands; no one seeks for God. All have turned aside; together they have become worthless; no one does good, not even one." From the cradle to college, any loving parent must exercise appropriate punishment upon their children for their own good without having to answer to the charge of being an unloving parent. This aligns with the testimony of Scripture. Our Heavenly Father chastens us because He loves us. The severity of punishment remains subject to the Divine Magistrate Himself, The Court, if you will. Fact: Should you happen to slip up and displease The Court with an arrogant disposition, you will likely face a harsher sentence. Thankfully, for our own sakes, God's indignation is only for a moment. Weeping may endure for a night, but joy comes in the morning! (Psalm 30:5).

This is hardly the end point of His love. True, He visits the iniquity of the fathers upon the children unto the third and fourth generation of them that hate Him. But this is only half the story. He extends mercy unto thousands of them that love Him and keep His commandments (Deuteronomy 5:9-10). God's mercy will always–positively always–outweigh His justice. Just consider:

Despite our tendencies to dabble in the affairs of the world, constantly antagonizing His grace, it is nevertheless because of the Lord's mercies that we are not consumed. Furthermore, the mercies of the Lord are from everlasting to everlasting. Best stated by F. B. Meyer, "There was never a time when God did not love you. Nor will there ever be a time when He will love you less– it is to everlasting." We are all too aware that David was no stranger to God's love, His grace, His longsuffering, His judgement, and yes, His mercy. His transgressions were anything but top secret. Nor was it classified information that he was a street-smart adulterer. Shrewd and calculating, David was precisely where he wanted to be when he saw what he liked and liked what he saw. In the spring, when the kings normally went out to war, David sent out Joab, his servants, and all the Israelites. They destroyed the Ammonites and attacked the city of Rabbah. But David stayed in Jerusalem. One evening David got up from his bed and walked around on the roof of his palace. While he was on the roof, he saw a woman bathing. She was very beautiful" (2 Samuel 11:1-3). Obviously, at such an ungodly hour of the night, nothing good can come from this. So, David sent his servants to find out who she was. A servant answered, "That woman is Bathsheba daughter of Eliam. She is the wife of Uriah the Hittite." As if to court disaster, David sends messengers to bring Bathsheba to him. "When she came to him, he had sexual relations with her. (Now Bathsheba had purified herself from her monthly period.) She then went back to her house, but she became pregnant and sent word to David, saying, "I am pregnant" (2 Samuel 11:5).

David: An Outright Murderer.

Not even the most jaw dropping Greek tragedy could compare with David's cunning, underhanded plot to cover up his sin. He shifts into damage control by sending for her husband Uriah with the intent of insisting that he return home and sleep with his wife. The attempt is unsuccessful. That evening Uriah again slept with the king's officers. Plan B: Invite Uriah over for a few drinks. In fact, get him drunk. After doing just that—getting Uriah drunk–the next morning David writes a letter to Joab and sends it by Uriah. In the letter David writes, "Put Uriah on the front lines where the fighting is worst and leave him there alone. Let him be killed in battle." Adultery. Murder. Lies. Cheating. Deception. Fraud. Double-Dealing.

At the same time, David was no better nor any worse than you or I. Romans 3:23 reminds us that we have "all sinned and come short." My position is firm: Nobody can determine the gravity of your "shortness." We all are short. Sure, some may have come shorter than others, but it really doesn't matter because the fact remains–we have all come short, period. I may not have committed murder, but if my dishonesty prevented you from being promoted, the fact is, I've come short. No matter what you've done, big sin or little lie, we're still short.

Look at Davd—the shortness pronounced by his iniquity yet the tallness of his humility. By the time the whole scandal had blown over, despite the backlash and domestic fallout, David yet proved himself to be a man after God's own heart. Gifted for adapting poetry to music– specifically to the chief musician upon stringed instruments–he establishes a career, an occupation, a legacy for Habakkuk to follow. (Habakkuk's lyrics are orchestrated in Chapter Seven).

Composed out of the embarrassing residue of his affair with Bathsheba and his calculated murder of her husband Uriah, David writes: "Have mercy upon me, O God, according to thy lovingkindness: according unto the multitude of thy tender mercies blot out my transgressions. Wash me throughly from mine iniquity, and cleanse me from my sin. For I acknowledge my transgressions: and my sin is ever before me" (Psalm 51:1-3).

Hurt, abuse, exploitation, injury, mistreatment, violation or victimization–our faith in God as the righteous judge can never be properly shaped by the debris of our past or present disappointments. This is irresponsible reasoning. It serves only to enlist more brazen attacks by the spirit of doubt. Other than the petitions we offer in supplication, we have no say whatsoever in the execution of God's justice. To be clear, we do not get to judge the fairness of God in Christ unto us based on the unregenerate shenanigans of the world. We do not, by any measure, possess so much as a smidgen of omniscience to debate the righteousness of God. We are humanly incapable of adjudicating what God does and aptly dismissed from having any say in how He does it. We are neither naturally nor spiritually intelligent enough to search out His understanding. We do not get to intermingle our carnal mentality with God's perfect judgement. We do not get to deliberate where man's shortcomings drop off and where God's grace picks up. We do not get to forecast how much rain falls on the just and the unjust. It falls equally. Get over it.

Personally, there is no question in my mind that from day one, our sense of right and wrong is molded by our parents and solidified by their own ethical example. This is why I thank God for my parents who taught me to love the Lord, to love God's people, to love the Church, to help people. They taught me it was wrong to smoke and drink and lie. My father told me, "If you see me bring alcohol into this house, you can drink it." But he never did. He said, "If you ever see me with a pack of cigarettes, that gives you the right to smoke." But he never did. He led by precept and example. He taught me to respect the house of God and to honor its leadership. He went on to warn me that "anytime you talk against the leadership of the Church, you are getting yourself into trouble with God." Until this day, with all of my heart, I truly believe this. And I thank God for the joy which has filled my life from embracing these principles my parents instilled within me.

When the rubber meets the road, we are responsible for our own actions. We cannot love the world (nor the things of the world) only to turn around and pin the blame on God's character whenever the world gets caught in the consequences of reaping what it has sown. Besides, when the Holy Ghost convicted you at the moment of your salvation, He doused your spirit with a plentiful helping of what is right and what is wrong. You know better. And whatever you were unsure of at the time was revealed in the holy precincts of your prayer life. When you failed to pray, your hearing became impaired and whatever once sounded ludicrous began to sound plausible: hence, the embodiment of doubt Keep praying, cease doubting. Grab the bull horn and replay it over and again: Cease doubting. Keep praying, and keep pressing. You may ask, "How do I get into the press?" "How do I find my way in this confusing race?" Let the Holy Spirit aid you in realigning your arguments, your debates, and most of all, your priorities, for "the letter killeth, but the spirit giveth life" (2 Cor. 3:6). Just look around; people are hurting everywhere. According to the U.S. Census, in 2020, there were 37.2 million people in poverty. That's approximately 3.3 million more than in 2019. Even more heartbreaking, "one in 7 adults say their households don't have enough to eat—a persistent crisis made worse by the pandemic" reports the *Washington Post*. Let's get focused on what's truly important—helping others who are in need.

One of my favorite Scriptures,

> "Blessed is he that considereth the poor: the Lord will deliver him in time of trouble. The Lord will preserve him and keep him alive; and he shall be blessed upon the earth: and thou wilt not deliver him unto the will of his enemies." (Psalm 41:1-2)

Also, take a moment to consider Deuteronomy 15:7-8,

> "If there be among you a poor man of one of thy brethren within any of thy gates in thy land which the Lord thy God giveth thee, thou shalt not harden thine heart, nor shut thine hand from thy poor brother: But thou shalt open thine hand wide unto him, and shalt surely lend him sufficient for his need, in that which he wanteth."

In other words, blessed is the one who has concern for the underdog. There is no shame in needing a hand-out and there is no need to be tight-fisted with those who do. Open thine hand unto the poor, to those who are needy. My entire world is completely devoted to giving, sharing, imparting, listening, forgiving, understanding, and offering to others whatever I can, whenever

I can. It is no strain for me to stop everything just to lend my time, my ear, my heart, my resources, my faith, my experiences, my trust (and just to frustrate my administrative staff), broadcast my cell number.

When you learn how to help people, and make it a part of your lifestyle, you will have no interest in frivolous "jury duty." Who is being helped by these ongoing debates anyway? It is not your place to prosecute, defend nor to exhaust all of your passion deliberating over what God allows. Your job is to get in line with God's Word, press on and press through. That's where your blessing is located—in the pressing. I've been on this journey a long time, and trust me, this race is not given to the swift nor to the strong, but it's given to the one who keeps pressing on. Don't get caught up in pointless debates. Don't get distracted. Don't get sidetracked. Don't get turned around. Stay encouraged. Because when it's all over, have no doubt, you shall wear a crown! You are not alone in your struggle to maintain a sound mind—we all go through tests and trials. Even right now, you may have questions about tomorrow, but take no thought for tomorrow—tomorrow will take care of itself. Just hang in there, endure to the end and get your prize. I cannot stress it enough— keep on pressing. Don't ever give up. Don't let anything or anybody—not your enemy, not your doubts—turn you around. Don't do it! Just keep going. Keep praying. Keep fasting. Through your pain, through your disappointments, through your heartache—keep pressing!

Stand up for what is right. Protest what is wrong. Be loud and proud if you must. But never lose sight of Who is in charge. "Repay no one evil for evil. Have regard for good things in the sight of all men. If it is possible, as much as depends on you, live peaceably with all men. Beloved, do not avenge yourselves, but rather give place to wrath; for it is written, "Vengeance is Mine, I will repay," says the Lord" (Romans 12:17-19).

Ultimately, the only true authority of justice is our Lord God Himself. Our job is to ask fewer probing questions—conduct far less cross-examination, and simply hold up our end of the arrangement. Not only must we recite God's mercy, but we must extinguish all doubt and confess it. Not only must we recite God's lovingkindness, but we must delete every speck of doubt by reporting it. And repeating it. And retelling it. Sounding the alarm upon His holy mountain! Despite all the petty details framed by our own contrariness, God alone is the Holy One Who has devised a plan for us to again be on good terms with Him (especially after Adam's fiasco in the Garden). So, come now, "let us reason together, saith the Lord: though your sins be as scarlet, they shall be as white as snow; though they be red like crimson, they shall be as wool" (Isaiah 1:18). This is the ultimate definition of what is "reasonable." This is the way it is. And it is what it is. It is fair. It is just. It is right. It is good. It is God.

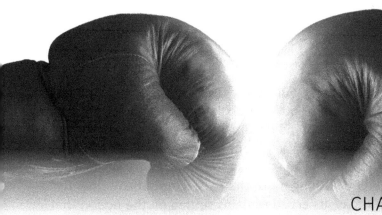
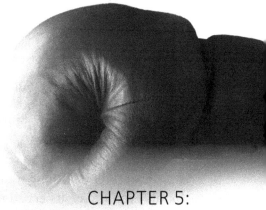

A BOUT WITH NEW THOUGHT

Yearning for something new? Something simple and easy on the mind? Something warm, comfy and emotionally pacifying to the soul, right? You already know: It absolutely cannot be too legalistic. Nothing too emotional, too complicated, too demanding or time-consuming. Maybe even something that operates on your terms and temperament. Perhaps something that gives you an equal voice in its protocols. Not too restrictive, not too stern, certainly not too structured and not too firm. Above all, you cannot tolerate any type of organized religion where you are being judged. God forbid.

As mentioned earlier, the time will come in your journey when you will be confronted, even tested, by a lie cleverly disguised as truth. This disguise will be accompanied by a voice which sounds credible, sensible and quite believable. (Gen. 3:5, The devil mixes in the truth. How could Eve be influenced by Satan if to believe the BIG LIE!) The lie will point you towards easy answers, feel good formulas, over-the-counter tips, clues, magical remedies, confessions, affirmations and witch hunts actually based on spiritual principles. All of its solutions will be simple. Painless. Effortless and convenient. Of course, its premise will carry no spiritual weight, but that will only matter to those committed to their personal spiritual growth. Are you? One such disguised lie showed up in 1878, then again in 1881, then again in 1914, in 1918, and again in 1925, asserting the exact time of

Christ's Second Coming. Such were the published predictions of the Watch Tower Bible and Tract Society. The lie however did its job. It achieved widespread deceit and lured away initially more than 200,000 "believers" self-identified as Jehovah's Witnesses who later adopted the teachings. This lie yet survives since it is propagated by nothing more than a single subtle moment of doubt. Even today, its creed remains settled on the notion that the destruction of the present world system at Armageddon is imminent, and that the establishment of God's kingdom over the earth is the only solution for all problems faced by humanity. A word of caution: If you are not up to speed on your biblical homework yet find yourself intrigued by unbiblically substantiated claims concerning the end of the world, the Second Coming of Christ or the galactic combat of Armageddon, you might want to avoid answering when they call at your door. Their worldwide membership of 8,000,000 need not increase by one more. Nevertheless, Habakkuk would certainly be less than flattered to learn that the Watchtower Society derived its name from his testimony!

Anyway, the disguised lie showed up again, only in a different costume, from the pulpit of The People's Temple, a ministry founded in Indianapolis, all the more heavily masqueraded by "good works"—soup kitchens, senior housing, drug rehabilitation programs, children's daycare, all promoting a social gospel. The chief accomplice: Jim Jones, masterfully skilled at the art of persuasion, contorting principles extracted directly from Scripture. Eventually, his followers–919 in total–followed him to the remote jungle of Guyana, South America. After their "paradise" failed in less than two years, on November 18, 1978, the faithful followers were urged to commit "revolutionary" suicide. Choosing death over the precious gift of life, they caved-in to the selfish proposition of doubt and succumbed to the lie. Only 87 members survived.

Once again, the disguised lie showed up as a rebranded mentality originally imported during the 19th Century. It touted a belief system emphasizing the interaction of "thought, belief, consciousness in the human mind, and the effects of these within and beyond the human mind." Here goes your warm, comfy, emotionally pacifying prescription for the soul. The spiritual movement is known as New Thought. Its counterpart is New Age. Both provide an easy escape from the reality that "in this world you will have trouble" (John 16:33).

Current followers of New Thought subscribe to a core set of beliefs:

1. God or Infinite Intelligence is "supreme, universal, and everlasting."
2. Divinity dwells within each person, that all people are spiritual beings.
3. The highest spiritual principle is loving one another unconditionally... and teaching and healing one another."
4. Our mental states are carried forward into manifestation and become our experience in daily living.

Both C. Alan Anderson and Deborah G. Whitehouse clarify, "New Thought concentrates on the power of the mind to heal and to prosper in a world in which all is mind. New Age especially extends this healing, prospering transformation to the entire planet, and with the inquisitiveness of youth, pokes its nose into numerous interesting corners, some clearly valuable, some questionable, in the process." The misguided context in which New Thought and New Age thrives is in the exercise of drawing in vibrations, mentally demanding the possible from the impossible. Yet it goes to such extremes as refusing medical treatment, electing instead to focus on self-spirituality which, they believe, leads to self-healing. New Thought specifically proposes "when you get in touch with the deeper levels of life, and yourself, that you tune into a vibration that is present throughout the universe." Supposedly, it is "not just about sitting and thinking, but it is about mind power, about heart power, about spiritual power; it is actually about being one with the divine and raising your thoughts from a human egocentric consciousness to a divine consciousness." In short, it is nothing more than a mouthful of carefully crafted nonsense.

The entire ideology is not only fundamentally flawed, but conceived from a disconnection with reality. We can easily see its motives played over and again by its soothing language, most appealing to those who desperately prioritize self-made success—entrepreneurship, stardom, extravagant wealth, and the list goes on. In fact, its followers subscribe to the central theory that "true human self-hood is divine." Here you have it! The ignorant, twisted, re-engineering of the premiere lie introduced by Satan. To the fragile minded, it beautifies the notion that through knowledge of good and evil "you will be like God" (Genesis 3:5). This is exactly how Satan attracted and captured the mind of man: by intriguing his desire to not only be like God but to have control of his own destiny. Nothing is new. It all traces back to the enticement which led to The Fall. New Thought uses this same old tactic to entice its current followers, and sadly, from the look of things, its growing by the minute.

The disguised lie made a cameo appearance in 2020 at the height of an already dangerous disinformation revolution. The cult, popularly known as Q-Anon, claims "there is a worldwide cabal of Satan-worshiping pedophiles who rule the world, essentially, and they control everything. They control politicians, and they control the media. They control Hollywood, and they cover up their existence, essentially." Just preposterous. Yet as outrageous as these claims may sound, they are perfectly plausible to the mind that has been massaged by doubt so consistently that a mental space has been reserved to receive "strong delusions, that they should believe a lie." How could this even happen? It happens easily "with all deceivableness of unrighteousness in them that perish; because they received not the love of the truth, that they might be saved" (2 Thess. 2:11-12).

From sunup until sundown, Habakkuk had to sit and watch doubt, an opportunist by the way, attempt to lure God's people, Judah, into the Chaldean worship of Anu (*regarded as the heaven-god*), Enlil (*the earth-god*) and Ea (*the water-god*). Though engaged in a bout with doubt himself, Habakkuk knew the risks involved. He knew the mere suggestion of such worship would be a blatant departure from the sharp directives of the Law—to place absolutely no other gods before the Lord God Who had brought their entire family out of Egypt. Throughout history, the Holy Spirit has scheduled more than a few showdowns to overturn this repetitive seduction into idolatry.

Who can erase from history the unforgettable showdown on Mount Carmel? If you recall, Mount Carmel had become a forsaken altar unto God and was now the ideal location for the worship of Baal. After several prophetic warnings, the moment of truth had arrived. The contest was on. The contestants were parked side by side. Water-filled trenches flowed around the altar. It was the Lord's altar, hand-built by Elijah with 12 stones: one for each of Jacob's sons. The big question: Upon which altar will God answer by fire? In unison, 450 prophets called on Baal. It was quite a sight! Standing alone, Elijah, inflexible and uncompromising, was calling on the name of God. Keep in mind, Baal was the supposed "god of lightening and fire," so this contest was right up his alley. Then, around the time of the evening sacrifice, Elijah stepped forward and said, "Lord, God of Abraham, Isaac, and Israel, today let it be known that You are God in Israel and that I am Your servant, and that I have done all these things at Your word. Answer me, Lord, answer me, so that this people may know that You, Lord, are God, and that You have turned their heart back." Then the fire of the Lord fell and consumed the burnt offering and the wood, and the stones and the dust; and it licked up the water that was in the trench. When all the people saw this, they fell on their faces; and they said, "The Lord, He is God; the Lord, He is God!" (1 Kings 18:36-39).

With a few striking similarities, Daniel had his turn at being irked by the idol-worshipping Chaldeans. They had not only influenced Nebuchadnezzar to toss his friends, Shadrach, Meshach, and Abednego into the fiery furnace, but were no doubt publicly embarrassed by the outcome. They were mortified by their failure to get Daniel and his friends to bow down and worship their gold statue.

The familiar fuel in each of these scenarios was the proposition made by none other than the nasty, insidious spirit of doubt itself. Who among us has not had to inhale its toxic fumes? I am no exception. By the grace of God, there is permanent picture in my memory of the day, the very hour, my mind was made up forever. It was the Fall of 1977, the Word of God came forth. It was full of power and precise. Suddenly, without any warning, an ear-splitting bell rang out in my spirit. It was sharp and piercing! The Holy Ghost was breaking through to the chambers of my heart, convicting me all the more beyond a shadow of doubt that "this is the word of faith, which we preach, That if thou shalt confess with thy mouth the Lord Jesus, and shalt believe in thine heart that God hath raised him from the dead, thou shalt be saved." Case closed. Match over. From that moment on, I knew my life, my walk, my relationship with my Lord and Savior would be forever compelled by the charge to put up a fight—the good fight of faith—and endure until the end.

That bell is going to ring again, any minute. When it does, be prepared to come out, not a loser, but a contender. Get warmed up to contend for the faith which was once delivered unto the saints. "For there are certain men crept in unawares, who were before of old ordained to this condemnation, ungodly men, turning the grace of our God into lasciviousness, and denying the only Lord God, and our Lord Jesus Christ. I will therefore put you in remembrance, though ye once knew this, how that the Lord, having saved the people out of the land of Egypt, afterward destroyed them that believed not" (Jude 3-5).

You already know the next move: The Hook. To pull off this move, reposition as much weight as you can to your stronger foot. Allow yourself to pivot and muster up some energy from your hips and upper body. Take your swing at doubt horizontally and then pivot your upper body to maximize the impact of the punch. When your faith is being confronted, and you take a stand for the Gospel of Jesus Christ, if your punch has no impact, your impact will have no influence. And influence is doubt's most reliable device for dragging spiritually underdeveloped believers off into the dark dungeon of deceit, often crippled at the knees and mentally incapable of again finding their footpath to The Way, The Truth and the Life. It will never be enough to be casually interested in the salvation Christ gives. You must get hooked!

To avoid being carried away with every wind of doctrine, always keep the name of Jesus on the tip of your tongue. All throughout my college years at Wayne State, I kept His name at the tip of my pencil as well. It was my own simple exercise of acknowledging Him in all my ways. From my very first semester as an undergraduate and ultimately to my Master's, I sketched out my own personal equation: At the beginning of exams, at the top left of the paper, I would write "INJ" (In the Name of Jesus). Then, at the conclusion of the exam, at the bottom right, I would write "INJA" (In the Name of Jesus, AMEN). What was that all about? It was about two principles: First, it was about being myself everywhere I went. My faith was in Jesus! My faith was not put into practice any less while on campus than in the sanctuary. Secondly, I refused to be "ashamed of the testimony about our Lord" (2 Timothy 1:8).

Taken together, New Age and New Thought are the perfect answer for those disinterested in putting up the stamina to walk with God according to the blueprint of His Word. It is the candy-coated dessert for the faint of heart. Maintaining your personal Christian life is work—hard work. There are no shortcuts, there are no quick fixes, there are no alternative options. You must do the work:

(1) **You must devote yourself to prayer**. Do it without ceasing—for, in practice, it is the antidote to doubting, so says Paul to Timothy regarding his ministry in Ephesus: "It is my will therefore that men pray everywhere, lifting up holy hands without wrath and doubting" (1 Timothy 2:9). There are no exceptions. I, as well, have a responsibility to God's people to stay plugged-in to Him, in season and out of season (1 Thess. 5:17). I am often reminded of this through the most charming of everyday circumstances. Yes, even when my grandson (not to mention any names) comes to the house and somehow manages to unplug my computer! I cannot waste any time, I must regroup those cords and cables and get immediately plugged back in. The same applies in the practice and habit of prayer.

For, you see, my connection to God through the power of prayer uploads the strength and toughness to that lifeline–that rope of hope—I may need to toss out to you one day when it seems your whole world is caving in on you; during those desperate moments when you feel yourself helplessly drowning in doubt. Catch hold! Your faith will pull you up every time. So, let's stay plugged-in!

(2) Accompanying your prayer life should be **a schedule of fasting**. Fasting produces discipline and builds resistance. Discipline and resistance: You will need plenty of both before climbing back into the ring against doubt. Sooner or later, if you intend to survive this Christian walk, all traces of doubt must be totally driven out. This is especially true since doubt itself may be classified as one of those "kinds" that come out only "by fasting and prayer." How fascinating that the principle of this storyline from Matthew 17, once again, defaults back to disbelief. The disciples were unable to rebuke the devil and cast him out of the young boy. When they privately came to Jesus and asked, "Why could we not cast him out?" Jesus said unto them, "Because of your unbelief; for verily I say unto you, if ye have faith as a grain of mustard seed, ye shall say unto this mountain, 'Remove hence to yonder place,' and it shall remove. And nothing shall be impossible unto you. However this kind goeth not out but by prayer and fasting" (Matthew 17:19- 21).

(3) **Submit yourself to persistent, focused study of God's Word**. Contrary to contemporary thinking, the Word of God is not due for updates to accommodate the progressive, liberal mentality of each new generation. His Word is fixed. It is non-negotiable. Plus, it digs deep and gets to the bottom of any doubts you may be entertaining (Hebrews 4:12). While responding to the murmuring of His disciples, Jesus called to their attention, "It is the Spirit that quickeneth; the flesh profiteth nothing. The words that I speak unto you, they are spirit, and they are life" (John 6:63).

(4) **Lose yourself in Worship**. True worship. True worship is worship of the Creator, *not* the Creation. True worship therefore is not for those tapped into the "energy of the universe"—but for those who are tapped into real time, since the hour has come "when the true worshippers shall worship the Father in spirit and in truth: for the Father seeketh such to worship Him. God is a Spirit: and they that worship Him must worship Him in spirit and in truth" (John 4:23-24). This is what you were created to do! When the Westminster Catechism asks, "What is the chief end of man?" The answer is clear cut: "Man's chief end is to glorify God, and to enjoy Him forever." To know this truth is also to know that there is no such "mind power, heart power or spiritual power" apart from the sanctifying power of the Holy Ghost. Both New Age and New Thought conveniently leave this out, unaware that to deny the work of the Holy Ghost is to also deny the very person of God with Whom the movement is allegedly striving to achieve divine unity. The entire principle is therefore self-contradicting and falls flat on its face. It can only survive where doubt abounds.

(5) **Pay Your Tithes First.** Please hear me: I did not say "pay your tithes." I said, "pay your tithes *first*." I know we live in what has become a "Me First" culture, but the tithe is the Lord's and it must always come first. You cannot expect to tap into the favor of God while committing robbery. How so? Wherein have we robbed Thee? In tithes and offerings. Therefore, it is your obligation as a true believer to "Bring ye all the tithes into the storehouse, that there may be meat in mine house, and prove me now herewith, saith the Lord of hosts, if I will not open you the windows of heaven, and pour you out a blessing, that there shall not be room enough to receive it." By the way, this includes "all the tithe of the land, whether of the seed of the land or of the fruit of the tree." This may seem somewhat insignificant when you are battling the strongholds of doubt, but it is actually very significant if you

intend to live an obedient life that is surrendered to the Lord. If you, in fact, profess to be holy, paying your tithes first comes along with that testimony, because plain and simple, "the tithe is holy" (Leviticus 27:30).

Ultimately, the entire conversation involving New Age and New Thought is hinged upon concrete, tangible evidence. This is not how faith works. Faith is the substance of things hoped for—no evidence! If evidence was required, the very definition of faith would fail by default. It is not by the power of the mind, nor positive thoughts attracting positive energy towards you, nor by the so-called "consciousness" of deity within you that any demand can be placed upon God to pour out His blessings. You can, however, place your ear against the door and hear the word of the Lord unto Zerubbabel, saying, "Not by might nor by power, but by My Spirit, saith the Lord of hosts" (Zechariah 4:6).

You will never be able to "attract enough positive energy" to move God to heal the condition of your body, your mind, your finances or the world. As for the earth and the universe, the earth is the Lord's and He alone possesses the power to shut up the heavens so there is no rain. He alone can send pestilence upon His people. At the same time, He stresses that "if my people who are called by my name shall humble themselves and pray; seek my face and turn from their wicked ways; then I will hear from heaven, I will forgive their sin and heal their land." Just do the work! For it is only by flexing our faith in the true and Living God through His Son Jesus Christ that the impossible becomes possible (Luke 18:27). Faith is like a muscle: The more you exercise it, the stronger it becomes. No vibrations. No sensations. No metaphysical electricity. No other way. No doubt.

CHAPTER 6

A BOUT WITH SIN

Habakkuk has a question on the table. And it is not a rhetorical one: "How long?" How long, O Lord, how long? Sounds familiar? Can you identify with where he is coming from? How long will our young brilliant African American men be gunned down on the streets for no reason? How long will the cycle of poverty devastate our communities? How long will the Church suffer persecution for doing all it can to bring aid and relief to those whom it serves? How long will the infestation of drugs and alcohol tear apart our homes? How long will rampant unemployment cause us to drown in debt? How long will the lethal hands of cancer wring the life out of our loved ones? How long must we sit back and watch God-fearing believers work, serve, give, sacrifice and pour out every last ounce of passion to build the kingdom, day after day, year after year, only to be taunted by the seemingly endless prosperity of the wicked? How long until You, O Lord, show up and do something? How long, O Lord, how long? Is there any question as to whether God will intervene? Is there any doubt? Whenever such groanings overtake you, one thing becomes obvious: The depth of your doubt has been intensified by the depth of your hurt. When the hurt runs deeply enough, it can drive you straight into the wilderness of sin.

From generation to generation, we are witnessing a volatile attack on the trustworthiness of Scripture as it addresses the problem of sin. This of course presents a much larger problem:

It metastasizes our understanding with questions about the entire Word of God, published with no shortage on the subject of sin. Suffice it to say, once we begin to entertain doubt from the very outstart of God's written record, we doubt everything which follows. The mischievous question, "Hath God said?" became the bait which landed us in this predicament in the first place: "Wherefore, as by one man sin entered into the world, and death by sin; and so death passed upon all men, for that all have sinned" (Romans 5:12). No matter how we break it down, all the strife, misery and suffering since that encounter in the Garden transpired from that one single act of enticement, framed as a question to elicit doubt–"Hath God said?" Such doubt can then be cleverly repurposed to question whether there are indeed actual consequences. This is what has Habakkuk in a tussle. He is patiently awaiting the onset of consequences for the rampant sins of the Chaldeans who are holding God's people against their will. Meanwhile, the risk of becoming blindsided by doubt is elevated all the more. From the opening scenes of Creation until today, the risk has continued to ramp up while the holy boldness of those charged with defending what God "hath said" is being gradually watered down.

As far as we know, Eve was minding her own business, but nevertheless became inquisitive of that tree, when she was approached by the serpent. God had spoken. The bait was dangled. Doubt was planted. The trap was set. Sin was committed. Just like that! When Ham came upon his father, Noah, in a stupor of drunkenness, he contrived it in his head that, instead of covering his father, he would expose him. Who would ever have thought things would turn out the way they did? Moses never thought he could possibly be found out when he murdered the Egyptian who had been taunting one of his fellow Hebrews. No one was around. The coast was clear. Doubt was planted. Sin was committed. Just like that! Moses had his quota of bad days. As he became increasingly aggravated in the wilderness, his aggravation got the best of him when he let out his frustration by striking that stone twice (after being specifically commanded by God to strike it only once). The water came gushing out and the congregation drank. But there remained consequences for his doubt: "Because ye believed me not, to sanctify me in the eyes of the children of Israel, therefore ye shall not bring this congregation into the land which I have given them" (Numbers 20:11-12). Considering all Moses had given of himself to lead his people out of slavery, through the winding maze of the wilderness and into Canaan, things did not have to go down like that. But they did.

While Sarah found God's promise in her old age amusing, Abraham believed God long enough to lift his eyes towards the stars, and "if thou be able to number them...So shall thy seed be" saith the Lord. Furthermore, the blessing "shall come forth out of thine own bowels." But we all know what happened. He doubted the process long enough to fall into the trap of sleeping with Sarah's handmaiden Hagar. That did not go over well, did it? Achan thought he was being smart when he secretly took the spoils from Jericho, despite God's warning that doing so would "make the camp of Israel liable to destruction and bring trouble on it" (Joshua 6:18-19). As for Uzzah, one may argue he was only trying to be helpful when the oxen which pulled the cart carrying the Ark of the Covenant began to shake. What did he do? Well, when they came to Nachon's threshing floor, he put forth his hand to the ark of God and took hold of it; for the oxen shook it (2 Samuel 6:6). For that split second, he doubted, resulting in the anger of the Lord being kindled against him. Right there, on the spot, God smote him for his error, and there he died by the ark of God. This is exactly what happens when doubt sets in—it heats up the impulse of sin. It draws you away. It impairs your judgement. James warns that none of us are immune from being lured away, but every man is tempted when he is drawn away of his own lust and enticed. Then when lust is conceived, it bringeth forth sin. And as for sin, when it is finished, it brings forth death (James 1:14-15).

The equation of sin looks like this:

The lust of the eyes—You like what you see (perhaps more than you should), and desire to have it.

The lust of the flesh—You like how it makes you feel (though it may not be yours to have). This is when perfectly natural desires become perverse, covetous, improper, unprincipled and immoral in the eyes of God.

The pride of life—You like how it inflates your ego, supplying your passions with "the things of the world" and swelling your demeanor with arrogance.

This vile enemy–doubt–tosses out two common punches: The first punch involves doubting God and everything connected with His Word. Buddhism says: "Doubt everything. Find your own light." This is a dangerous principle and has no place in the contemplations of a believer. Doubt, being the opportunist it is, will play upon the believer's weaknesses with almost sociopathic disregard for their weak condition. No season in the believer's life is more vulnerable to these attacks than when the believer is facing an storm. We can see one of these storms unfolding in Matthew Chapter 14. After a satisfying meal where Christ Himself fed the multitude, Jesus invited His disciples into the boat to cross over to the other side of the lake. By the time night had fallen and the boat had drifted far out from the shoreline into the sea, suddenly, the wind picks up speed. More and more, the wind accelerates until it begins to howl. The howling winds are now tossing heavy surges of rain everywhere, thrashing against the ship as the waves forcefully crash up into the vessel, jolting it uncontrollably out of sail. Panic on deck! The disciples are in a frenzy, bumping into each other. They are staggering in pitch blackness, zero visibility, unable to see where they are going or what they are doing. No relief in sight. No help to be found.

They are desperate. Totally petrified in the face of doom, entirely in God's hands. Was this the end? After all of the intimate hours spent in the personal company of Jesus, was this really happening to them? Were they really going to go out like this? Then, at about four o'clock in the morning, Jesus came toward them walking on the water. At last! Were they relieved? Nope. They were terrified! "A ghost!" they said, crying out in terror. Between the crashing of the waves, they could hear His voice reassuring them, "Do not be afraid." No other voice at that frantic moment could have been more distinct, "Do not be afraid!" Sounds reassuring, right? Peter then asks the most startling question of his life–the question that would become more rattling than the winds beating up against the ship. He somehow works up enough nerve to ask, "Master, is that you?" Far be it for the disciples to snap back with a bit of up-to-the-minute sarcasm, "No, it is a ghost!" Instead, they just watched the whole thing play out. "Come ahead" Jesus again reassuring him that it is safe to step out on the water. For one bold second, Peter steps out on the water and walks towards Jesus. But it was short-lived when he felt the waves churning beneath him, looked down, lost his nerve, felt himself sinking–and sinking quickly—wails out a cry, "Master, save me!" We may never know if Jesus was more disappointed or annoyed by Peter's failure to combat his doubt and walk to Him on the water. Imagine Jesus shaking His head as He reached down, grabbed Peter's hand and pulled him up into the ship. What we do know is once they both climbed into the ship, the wind began to die down. The other disciples in the boat, having watched the whole thing, worshiped Jesus, saying, "This is it! You are God's Son for sure!" (verses 32-33). Peter, dripping wet, worn out and no doubt gasping for breath must now face the inevitable question, "Brother Peter, faint-heart, what got into you?" Doubt.

The second common punch involves doubting the consequences of doubting God. In her wildest dreams, did Sarah ever think her decision (and Abraham's willing participation) would result in the embarrassment of a dysfunctional domestic showdown? Did Moses ever conceive that, after all he had to tolerate from the children of Israel in the wilderness, that he himself would never see the Promised Land? Did Achan give it even a second thought that his sin would reap destruction upon Israel? Did Uzzah ever really think that the site of Nachon's threshing floor would become his own crime scene? Keep in mind, it only took a split second for him to become enticed by a lie and lured away. We have all been there.

How do you find your way back? You cannot do it on your own. You need help. We all do. Happily, help is available! "But the

Helper, the Holy Spirit Whom the Father will send in My name, He will teach you all things, and remind you of all that I said to you" (John 14:26).

The Holy Ghost takes you back to the place where you first believed. He convicts—He digs out all leftover residue of doubt—and realigns your heart with the solid truth of your personal faith. In moments of discouragement and vulnerability, few refrains, so simple, touch my heart as those penned by Andrae Crouch,

> *Take me back, take me back, dear Lord*
> *To the place where I first received You*
> *Take me back, take me back, dear Lord*
> *Where I first believed.*

It is therefore hardly enough to have an open mind, you must have an open heart. This is where conviction goes to work. It works upon the altar of your heart. Remember, whenever the heart is opened to the sound of the Gospel, pricked to confess the Lord Jesus Christ as Savior under the convicting power of the Holy Ghost, this touch overpowers the pull of doubt. No longer can there be any question that God has raised Christ Jesus from the dead. This is the remedy God has prescribed. There is no other way to again stand in good graces with God. There is no other way to come before God except on His terms, since without faith it is impossible to please Him, "for he that cometh to God must believe that he is, and that he is a rewarder of them that diligently seek Him" (Hebrews 11:6).

For this round, you have none other than the Holy Ghost, Who Himself has a weapon all His own: conviction. The wonderful thing about conviction is its accuracy. You cannot duck, you cannot dodge. When it swings, it never misses. The most damaging blow to doubt is handed down from the power of the Holy Ghost to CONVICT. Doubt can show all of its true disingenuous characteristics, but when conviction punctures the human heart, it is technically a wrap! TKO. Game over. In the afterglow of Pentecost, when Paul had cast out a spirit of divination from a female slave, and thrown into jail, after a night of lifting up songs of praises which aroused an earthquake, the Philippian Jailer rushed in and fell trembling before Paul and Silas. He brought them out and asked, "Sirs, what must I do to be saved?" Hence, the outburst of a convicted heart! They replied, "Believe in the LORD Jesus, and you will be saved—you and your household" (Acts 16:30-31).

Habakkuk is sensitive to sin and he is slowly running out of patience watching it seemingly run rampant and unchecked. Deep in his heart he knows, down the road—preferably sooner than later—there must be some consequences. Still, he was not prepared to yield to the temptations of doubt. Besides, certain things are just downright unaffordable. You cannot afford to forget that you believe that the Lord is not willing that any should perish, but that all should come unto repentance. You cannot afford to forget that you believe in miracles, healing, unconditional grace and complete deliverance. The very God Who is Holy is the very God Who will deliver His people from the congestion of Chaldean oppression. I, for one, can never afford to forget that I am saved and I am sanctified, filled with God's precious Holy Ghost and that with a mighty burning fire. And I do speak in tongues as the Spirit gives utterance!

You cannot afford to forget that sin is the sequel to doubt. It is expensive. Its wages equal death. Its definition has not changed, God still hates it. It has not achieved any worthwhile benefits lately. Nothing good can ever come of it. It is not open to interpretation. All unrighteousness is sin. It is not extinct. What was sin yesterday is sin today. What is sin today will be sin tomorrow. It is not subjective. Sin is whatever God says it is. It carries no life-giving properties. The soul that sinneth shall die. It is progressive. If only a hint of doubt can get you to lie, then not much more can convince you to steal. Lying and stealing—it is all sin. Sin is not a virus that runs its course over a three-day weekend. It is a disease that is treated only through repentance. Sin is no respecter of persons. It does not identify only with gangsters, prostitutes and drug dealers. It winks at the pious, the praiser and the prophet. Sin does not just gradually go away. It must be washed away. Its dirty particles come out in the rinse when the blood of Jesus is applied. Sin is not old fashioned. It is up to speed with every platform from YouTube to Facebook to Twitter to Instagram to TikTok. Even while you are ministering the Word of God, pouring out your heart, doing all you can to encourage and impart hope to those who are desperately clinging to your words over social media, doubt will show up and show out with all kinds of negative feedback posted in the "live chat." (Lord, help me–I did it again! I said, "chat room." Sorry, Kierra. Your Dad meant to say "comments" honestly).

Sin is not cute either. In the eyes of God, it is appallingly ugly. Sin cannot be outsmarted. It knows what you like and has the resources to get it to you. Sin is not harmless. It is utterly destructive. Sin never knows when to shut up. It will keep you up all night until you talk yourself into doing the wrong thing. Sin will snatch you up, hang you out to dry and snitch you out (Numbers 32:23). Sin adds to your weight. In turn, it scrutinizes your eligibility for your weight class. Therefore, "let us lay aside every weight, and the sin which doth so easily beset us, and let us run with patience the race that is set before us" (Hebrews 12:1).

The Hebrew writer forewarns that the sin which so easily besets us is aggravated by the weight which comes along to wear us down. Sin and weight. Weight and sin. It is a duo which chips away at our spiritual durability until, at the bare bone, hope nudges us to ask, "What must I do to *stay* saved?" How do I sustain my salvation? How do I avoid falling out of the boat again? How do I measure up to the expectations of a holy God? What does it really mean to be holy? What does it really mean to be sanctified? What does it mean to be sanctified *and* holy? The answer is not complicated. It means what it has always meant.

To be *holy* is to be set aside by God; to be distinct from the world. It is an appeal to prepare your mind for action, to keep sober in spirit, to fix your hope completely on the grace to be brought to you at the revelation of Jesus Christ. Furthermore, "as obedient children, do not be conformed to the former lusts which were yours in your ignorance, but like the Holy One who called you, be holy yourselves also in all your behavior; because it is written, 'You shall be holy, for I am holy'" (1 Peter 1:13–16).

To be *sanctified* is to be set apart, called out, separated, singled out for God's use in acceptable service. To be sanctified *and* holy is to be submitted to the experience of one attribute (*personal sanctification*) seasoning the other (*personal holiness*) for your own good in the eyes of God so that your whole spirit, soul and body are preserved blameless unto the coming of our Lord Jesus Christ (1 Thess. 5:23). Anything less means living at risk of yielding to temptation. To be clear, temptation itself is not the sin; but rather the *act of yielding* is sin.

As the legend goes, told by Stanley Stuber, back when Sing Sing Prison in New York housed women, a riot had erupted. Soon the entire facility was spinning into chaos. The prison matron was hysterically pulling upon whomever she could for help to calm the women. It was well known that a revolt by the women prisoners was far more difficult to contain than a revolt by the men. Suddenly, "a clear, strong voice rose above the clamor and crying of the rebellious prisoners, *"Yield not to temptation, For yielding is sin; Each victory will help you, Some other to win. Fight manfully onward, Dark passions subdue; Look ever to Jesus, He'll carry you through!"* Suddenly, a peaceful hush stilled the riot. One by one the inmates joined in the song until as one they formed a line and marched quietly back to their cells."

As already expressed, you cannot do it alone. You cannot overcome the temptation of sin by yourself. You must reach out for help:

Ask the Savior to help you,
Comfort, strengthen, and keep you;
He is willing to aid you,
He will carry you through.

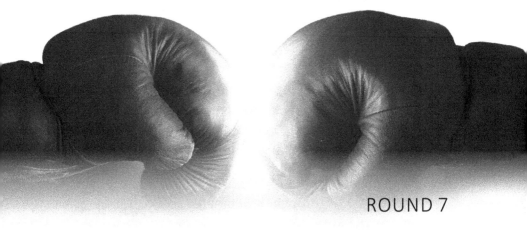

A BOUT WITH BELIEF

At its core, a bout with doubt is a bout with belief. Therefore, whenever you climb into the ring with doubt, the strength needed to pull off a win is not your own. You will never be able to keep up the fight. You will wear down in no time without the aid of your Helper. Without Him, you are unable to make any confession unto salvation. It is impossible since, "no man can say that Jesus is the Lord, but by the Holy Ghost" (1 Cor. 12:3). During those dry spells however, when you must rely upon what you know despite what you feel, things can become rocky. But you have come too far to drop out now.

Stay in the ring! You still have what it takes to walk away with the title in your weight class. Besides, you have yet to exhaust all of your best maneuvers. There is still the "uppercut"– another intense blow that demands your full body weight. It's a move similar to a "strike" I remember seeing whenever my Dad would take my brother Ethan and I to watch wrestling at the Cobo Arena. As you throw it, your legs, shoulders and feet should all swerve away at the same time, in the same direction. Caution—avoid leaning back or hopping. (If you happen to lean back, make sure you lean not to your own understanding). Keep your feet planted. This will keep you clear of being thrown off guard. Fair question: How do I stay planted when I am exhausted, wasted, spent, ready to drop? Why bother going at another round when all I want is for this scuffling to just end? Enough is enough.

Habakkuk has basically the same questions. He is nearly on the edge of being mentally undone, watching his people fidget under the trap of this wicked, ungodly nation. But he has some growing to do! He is about to learn a life lesson—The fulfillment of God's promises to His people is not attained by manipulating His hand with impatience—spiritual pouting—but it is settled in Christ Jesus (2 Cor. 1:20). Through His ultimate sacrifice, Christ rescues us from the climate of sin's influence so that we are transported unharmed into a safety zone, a healing place, indeed a cheerful place. So cheer up! Awaken your spirit and flip the script! Flip the script on such questions as, "Why don't you do something about this? Why are you silent now? This outrage! Evil men swallow up the righteous and you stand around and watch!" (Habakkuk 1:13). When the script is flipped you will instead ask, "Why art thou cast down, O my soul? And why art thou disquieted in me? Hope thou in God: for I shall yet praise him for the help of his countenance" (Psalm 42:5). Oh yes, when the script if flipped, you will arrive at the place where you'll discover that this is not the time for bellyaching, this is not the time for being a crybaby, pouting like an adolescent or throwing a temper tantrum, but this is the time to square your shoulders and prepare to win this fight!

God sees the perspiration streaming down your face. Hold still and let Him wipe it away so you can clearly recognize your true opponent. For too long you have been wasting your energy taking swings at the wrong opponent. You are not in a bout with flesh and blood. You are in a bout with principalities, powers, rulers of the darkness of this world. You are in a bout with spiritual wickedness in high places on assignment to throw you off your game by planting, watering and cultivating seeds of doubt.

Doubt has done its homework. It already knows your weight class. Given your status as a seasoned, mature, Spirit-filled, battle-scarred believer, doubt already knows it cannot toss out any frivolous claims which, at this point in your life, are far beyond your stretch of patience to amuse. Doubt will not present someone in your weight class with arguments over the ceremonial formulas for water baptism, or the ethnicity of our Savior or the New Testament ruling concerning the Sabbath. We need not lay over again "the foundation of repentance from dead works, and of faith toward God" but rather "leaving the principles of the doctrine of Christ, let us go on unto perfection" (Hebrews 6:1). In other words, let's not continue repeating the same issues over and over again. Your weight class is well beyond those arguments. However, doubt will cleverly introduce questions which challenge the fundamental substance of your personal faith: If God's grace is represented in His unmerited favor, and if Christ is The Bread of Life, The Light of the World, The Door of the Sheep, The Resurrection and the Life, not to mention The Good Shepherd and The True Vine, why are you suffering? Why are you struggling? Why are you breaking your back and getting nowhere? Why are you living from paycheck to paycheck? Better yet, if you are able to speak with the tongues of men and of angels, with prophetic powers, understanding all mysteries and all knowledge, and if you have all faith so as to remove mountains; if your soul is prospering, why are *you* not prospering?

Before you swing back, you must do what wisdom commands: look at the source. Once you know the source of the dispute, you will know the target of the dispute. The source is Satan. The target is The Kingdom. Take note of the details: *Principalities* are aimed at controlling and bringing down nations. *Powers* seek out to possess humans. *Rulers of the darkness of this world* have command over Satan's worldly affairs and *spiritual wickedness in high places* exists to overthrow religions. Hence, when doubt is ready to make its move, its central target is the foundation of your faith.

Even those whom you love can be easily lured away. Some will break loose. Others will return with warped concepts twisted into ideas directly antithetical to their upbringing. When our children go off to college, they become ripe targets for Satan's rhetoric. It infiltrates their minds which are now open to fresh ideologies, philosophies and contemporary systems of belief—or non- belief. In Bob Smietana's Special for USA TODAY *"College Students Divided on God, Spirituality"* he identifies Daniel Jansouzian, a junior at Middle Tennessee State University in Murfreesboro, who runs a start-up Pentecostal ministry at the School. Jansouzian states that many students grew up attending church but no longer attend. Being religious now, he says, is a conscious choice. His group runs four bible studies and a weekly worship service. "We want to reach those who lost their faith or who are looking for something to believe in."

How interesting to turn back a few pages and recall that an entire revolution of nonbelievers stemmed from an elementary school controversy stirred up by one defiant parent. Eventually, she would become a household name: Madalyn Murray O'Hair. Does that name strike a bell? She is the rebellious outspoken founder of the largest organized atheist movement in the United States, American Atheists. Waging an all-out war against prayer and bible reading in schools, citing the practice as unconstitutional, violating the separation of Church and State, the sting of her 30-year campaign against the existence of God is felt today. Fiercely educated, astonishingly intelligent, though steadily unemployed and likewise unmarried with two children born out of wedlock, suicidal at times, kicked out of Mexico, even rejected by the Soviet Union, she carried her cause to the steps of the United States Supreme Court.

On June 17, 1963, the Supreme Court issued its ruling: "We repeat and again reaffirm that neither a State nor the Federal Government can constitutionally force a person 'to profess a belief or disbelief in any religion.' Neither can it constitutionally pass laws or impose requirements which aid all religions as against non-believers, and neither can it aid those religions based on a belief in the existence of God as against those religions founded on different beliefs."

We already know that only the fool has said in his heart there is no God. From the outbreak of this revolution of unbelief, doubt was nonetheless effective at creating a deep, painful and unsightly incision into our concept of God Himself. The daughter of Presbyterian and Lutheran parents, armed with a law degree, O'Hair harps on and on, "An atheist is a person who questions every type of authority" she asserts, "[and this is] important because if we can, without blinking an eye, question the ultimate authority, God, Who must be obeyed, then we can question the authority of the State, we can question the authority of the university structure, we can question the authority of our employer, we can question anything."

When O'Hair emerged onto the scene with her noisy message, it was perfectly timed. Her rhetoric coincided with the rise of the counter-culture movement of the 60s. Among this group of "hippies" nothing was sacred; everything was questioned, everything was challenged. She waged her war day-in and day-out. Finally, after 20 years of confrontations, death threats and legal battles, O'Hair withdrew slowly from public view, surrounded only by her younger son Garth and granddaughter. Then one night in 1980, for her older son, Bill, whose childhood was upstaged by his mother's relentless drive against prayer in schools after hearing the Lord's Prayer recited in class each morning, everything was about to change. Really change.

In his book, *My Life Without God*, Bill Murray recounts his experience,

> "On the night of January 24, 1980, an unusual event changed my life. I went to bed and, not long after falling asleep, experienced a consuming nightmare of unmentionable horror. Suddenly, the nightmare was sliced in half by a mighty, gleaming sword of gold and silver. The two halves of the nightmare peeled back as if a black-and-white photograph had been cut in half. A great winged angel stood with the sword in his hand. The blade of the sword pointed down, making it resemble a cross."

> He goes on, "The tip of the sword's blade touched an open Bible. Then I awoke, realizing that my quest for the truth would end within the pages of the Holy Bible, the very book my family had helped ban from devotional use in the public schools of America. It was no doubt a chilling encounter. Wide-awake, I climbed out of bed, dressed, and drove into San Francisco. I believed this dream

had told me two things. First, the answers to most if not all of my personal problems and dilemmas were in the book the sword had touched, the Bible. Second, only through the cross would I be able to conquer these problems." Finally, he retraces his steps, "I drove to my apartment and read the book of the Bible written by the great physician Luke. There I found my answer—not the book itself, but Jesus Christ. I had heard many times in various places that all one needed to do was admit guilt and ask Jesus in. I had not made that one step, to ask Him into my heart. And I knew I must. On the morning of January 25, I got down on my knees, confessed my sins, and asked Christ into my life. God was no longer a distant "force." I now knew Him in a personal way. Within days my life and attitudes began to change. I read in the Bible that anything asked in Jesus' name in prayer would be answered. My hatred began to vanish as the love of Christ took over my being. I no longer intensely hated my mother. Now I really wanted to be able to love her, whereas before I had only wanted revenge. I began to see my mother for what she truly was, a sinner, just like me. She blamed God and humankind, rather than herself, for her personal sins and inadequacies. She had demanded things of God, and when He had refused her demands, she had fought with Him openly. Now I looked back at the devastation. My family, and particularly my mother and myself, had left a path of ruin behind us—ruined ideals, ruined lives. We had marched over both in quest of a victory that could not be won."

What a testimony! Today, Bill is a born-again, Spirit-filled, Baptist minister. From a childhood fed by lies, a household of godlessness, and the wicked influence of a shameless mother who led him into complete darkness—truth prevailed! Case closed. When the authority of the Gospel witness shows up, doubt is forced to back down. On the Day of Pentecost, Peter was left with no choice but to immediately extinguish the very suggestion that the disciples in the Upper Room were drunk at 9 o'clock in the morning. He had to squash every doubt that this experience—this visible manifestation of the Holy Ghost—was anything other than the fulfillment of prophecy placed in the mouth of Joel 700 years earlier.

Peter stood up, took his time and made it plain,

> "Ye men of Judea and all ye who dwell in Jerusalem, be this known unto you, and hearken to my words. For these are not drunken as ye suppose, seeing it is but the third hour of the day; but this is that which was spoken by the prophet Joel: 'And it shall come to pass in the last days, saith God, I will pour out My Spirit upon all flesh; and your sons and your daughters shall prophesy, and your young men shall see visions, and your old men shall dream dreams. And on My servants and on My handmaidens I will pour out in those days My Spirit, and they shall prophesy. And I will show wonders in heaven above, and signs in the earth beneath—blood and fire and vapor of smoke. The sun shall be turned into darkness, and the moon into blood before that great and notable Day of the Lord come."

And here is my favorite part: "And it shall come to pass that whosoever shall call on the name of the Lord shall be saved" (Acts 2:14-21).

There is no opponent on earth which can defeat the power of truth. When your backup arrives, that is, "When the Spirit of truth comes, he will guide you into all the truth, for he will not speak on his own authority, but whatever he hears he will speak, and he will declare to you the things that are to come" (John

16:13). The closer your encounter with doubt, the tougher your blow to its head. When Christ died, He crushed the devil's head and despite the prophetic fulfillment of His resurrection, Thomas insisted, "Unless I see the nail marks in his hands and put my finger where the nails were, and put my hand into his side, I will not believe" (John 20:25). This was a sample case enlarged all the more by Christ's warning later in Matthew 24, "For there shall arise false Christs, and false prophets, and shall shew great signs and wonders; insomuch that, if it were possible, they shall deceive the very elect." In short, a little doubt now can turn you into a big fool later! To avoid so great a tragedy, barricade the door of your right mind, let no corruption seep in, leaving no room for such deception to overtake you.

Tragically, O'Hair was kidnapped and murdered along with her younger son and granddaughter. She lost her lifelong inner struggle with doubt and, unlike Bill, never recovered. She was never quite able to clinch her fists at its irrational mind games nor strangle the life out of its stronghold. Doubt got the best of her and revealed the worst. In fact, the very dirt which covers her unmarked grave in an undisclosed location still retains the texture of doubt, since it was her request that upon her burial, no prayers would be said. Her legacy is etched into the most frightening chambers of our memory as "The Most Hated Woman in America." This did not have to happen. She carried a hardened heart straight to the grave. This brand of stubbornness is no light matter. It is a serious symptom which requires emergency attention. A chronically hardened heart will eventually cause you to get stuck in the mire, leaving a permanent blemish on your life story– again, if you give in. I implore you with all my heart, do not give in. You have come too far to throw up your hands and just walk away. If you must throw up your hands, throw them up in worship.

All Habakkuk wanted was to hear back from God. He was listening, and very carefully, for an answer from the voice of God alone and no other. He knew God would surely answer. You and I know as well, because God is yet speaking. Silence from heaven has not fallen upon the earth as it did in the years following Malachi's last recorded prophecy. We are not destitute for a Word from the Lord. Jesus is standing at the door of your heart knocking. The day you hear His voice, please do not do the unthinkable. Do not harden your heart. The last thing you need is to become a victim of a hardened heart. In case no one has told you, let me say it again—You are better than that. So much better, by far. You are a valuable vessel endowed with the power of choice. The power of choice is inextricably bound to the gift of life. Every single time you choose faith over doubt, you are choosing life over death. Literally, "I call heaven and earth to record this day against you that I have set before you life and death, blessing and cursing. Therefore, choose life, that both thou and thy seed may live" (Deuteronomy 30:19).

That choice has not expired. With the dawning of each new day, with the awakening to every new sunrise, this choice is set before you. And the choice is all yours. Perhaps yesterday you chose to believe God for your complete physical healing over the insinuations of doubt. Why should today be any different? Perhaps yesterday you placed your teenager in the hands of the Lord, choosing to believe God to turn them around from a wayward, destructive path, despite evidence to the contrary presented by doubt. Should today be any different? Maybe you have endured so much pain, so much anguish, so much disappointment and so much heartache that it has rejuvenated you to "suffer affliction with the people of God" than to enjoy the pleasures of sin for a season. When the season ends, the pleasures fizzle out. Once the pleasures are cut down and wither away, doubt rises back up.

Therefore, Jesus' invitation still stands, "Behold, I stand at the door and knock." If you would just hear my voice and open the door to your heart, here is what you can look forward to: (1) "I will come in." (2) "I will dine with you." (3) "You will dine with Me" (Revelation 3:20).

Where do you stand? I cannot stress it enough—you are better than the spectacle doubt is attempting to make of you. Things are not always as they appear. The grass is not always greener across the road. Look beyond the road, beyond the fields, beyond the artificial pastures. In fact, look beyond the hills from whence comes your help! Drown out the noisy nonsense of doubt and declare that all of your help comes from the Lord. Never mind what doubt is telling you, the Lord will not suffer your foot to be moved. He slumbers not. He sleeps not. Whose report are you going to believe anyway? What has doubt done for you lately? Where has it gotten you? Just look at O'Hair. She ended up in a ditch. Dead. Dismembered. No one deserves to die like this. Everyone deserves their moment in the ring, in the spotlight, in a face-off with doubt. She confronted everyone and everything except doubt itself. She believed whatever it suggested to her, opening the gateway for an army of know-it-all unbelievers to rise up and demand to be heard. Decidedly, she made a career of questioning everything, everyone and every authority only to become the most pitiful example of one who was "ever learning, yet never coming into the knowledge of the truth." The danger of her example has not faded into oblivion.

Questioning everything is still the perfect way to dig yourself into a hole. It remains frightening to imagine where we would be if there was no healing beyond the bruises of doubt. But there is. God be praised! There is still time. Hallelujah! There is still hope. There is an earnest breaking up of that stony heart when Jesus is welcomed-in to alleviate your pressure, restore a steady heartbeat, remove the smog caused by spiritual glaucoma, break through every fetter and set you free to achieve great success without the nuisance of doubt tapping you on the shoulder every other minute. If you absolutely must turn your head—turn to God, resist the devil and he will flee from you!

Again, keep building up that resistance. You cannot bow out of the race now. You're not a quitter, you're a winner. Quitters never win and winners never quit! If you can see the prize ahead, then you can also feel the pressure that comes with it. And when the pressure is on, all roads may very well lead back to the initial question: How do I stay planted when I am exhausted, wasted, spent, ready to drop? Why would I even go at another round of this when all I want is for this scuffling to just end? Enough is enough. Rest assured, after six full rounds with this vile enemy called "doubt", you are not alone. Your cries are not falling on deaf ears. Your agony is not being tuned out. Above all, you have not been rejected nor isolated. You and Habakkuk are partners of purpose.

To recapitulate, Habakkuk's question—just like yours—was not a rhetorical one. The prophet genuinely needed to satisfy his spirit by awaiting and obtaining God's answer: "How long?" The scene was critical. The nation was falling apart. The pagans were taking over. How could these things be allowed to happen? How could God allow the triumph of evil over righteousness? He cries out, "O Lord, you are too holy to even look at sin." And yet you seem to tolerate these calamities that are taking place before my every eyes. What exactly is going on? What to do? First of all, "I will stand upon my watch, and set me upon the tower, and will watch to see what he will say unto me, and what I shall answer when I am reproved." Then, he becomes outright indignant, "I have shaken my fist in the face of God, I have demanded an answer–an explanation–as to why He tolerates all of this evil. Until He answers me, I will be right here upon my watchtower–strong winds, torrential storms, drought or desolation, I shall not be moved. In fact, I refuse to even budge." Thus he waited. And waited. He waited more. He waited still. A few thunderstorms here and there, but he waited. Sure enough, at long last, "the Lord answered me, and said, Write the vision, and make it plain upon tables, that he may run that readeth it. For the vision is yet for an appointed time, but at the end it shall speak, and not lie: though it tarry, wait for it; because it will surely come, it will not tarry."

How we love to hear the promises of God. But when God is slow to fulfill the promises, when the Lord tarries, we become impatient, restless, contentious and even angry with God. God says to Habakkuk, "Take it easy. Calm down a bit. My promise have I spoken and it is still valid. It may tarry, but it will surely come to pass." By the time Habakkuk comes back in Chapter 3, verse 16, something has happened. He has heard from God. His testimony is captivating, "When I heard this, every muscle in my body reacted. My belly trembled; my lips quivered at the voice of the Lord. Immediately, I saw myself for who I really was. It was so real and so raw that rottenness entered into my bones. I could not stop trembling within myself as I nearly tripped over myself searching for rest in the day of trouble, knowing full well that it is only a matter of time before He will invade our attackers with His troops."

The reaction of Habakkuk to the Word of God is classic. It is in fact the uniform reaction of those in the Old Testament when they encountered the True and Living God. Habakkuk speaks of trembling in the presence of God. He speaks of seeing himself as he really is. Can you not hear Isaiah describing how "the house was filled with smoke" and his immediate reaction? "Woe is me! For I am undone; because I am a man of unclean lips" (Isaiah 6:4-5). Isaiah's lips were quivering. He saw himself for who he really was. Habakkuk's lips are quivering. Have you ever seen the lips of a little child when they are about to cry and doing everything in their power to stop from crying? As the parent, you already know it is a losing battle because those lips are starting to quiver, and in a matter of seconds, the tears will come. This is what is happening to Habakkuk. He cannot hold it in. The Word of God has taken his heart into custody. He is overwhelmed. He is sobbing, "My belly trembled. My lips quivered. And a sense of rottenness entered my bones." Then, as if rising out of the ashes of his own pitifulness, he utters the charge quoted three times in the New Testament. "But the just shall live by faith" (Habakkuk 2:4). That is, the righteous will live by trust! So, get down from your watchtower, Habakkuk, and trust Me!

Like a sudden rush of cool air, the essence of Habakkuk's trust in God breaks forth, rupturing every barrier of doubt, gushing forcefully into his timeless hymn of hope, help and healing: "Although the fig tree shall not blossom, neither shall fruit be in the vines; the labour of the olive shall fail, and the fields shall yield no meat; the flock shall be cut off from the fold, and there shall be no herd in the stalls: Yet I will rejoice in the Lord, I will joy in the God of my salvation." What say ye? Though my business fails miserably, though the stock market crashes and the economy is in ruins, though the nation is conquered by foreign invaders, my home goes into foreclosure, my children abandon me—nevertheless, I will rejoice in the God of my salvation. You may ask, how can I go on? How can I recover from the agony of my patience being stretched to the limit? How can I move past these personal failures? How can I move past the wickedness of these Chaldeans? How can I move past these nagging temptations that mess with my faith? How do I walk past all of these injustices? How do I come down from my watchtower, pick myself up, get past what I see and stand upon what I truly know in my heart? Habakkuk testifies that the way has already been made, the strength has already been supplied, the endurance has already been outfitted just for me, for He has made my feet "like the feet of deers" super-charged with the stability, the tenacity and the power to walk upon my high places. Just wait for it. Again, I say, wait for it!

You cannot sing such an hymn out loud until you first hear it from within. It must first puncture the steel barriers which lead to the deep places within your heart and simmer in your spirit until the molecules of doubt completely evaporate. Then you are free to sing! "Although the fig tree shall not blossom, neither shall fruit be in the vines; the labour of the olive shall fail, and the fields shall yield no meat; the flock shall be cut off from the fold, and there shall be no herd in the stalls: Yet I will rejoice in the Lord, I will joy in the God of my salvation."

Again, I say, rejoice! Stay in the ring. Swing back. Remain planted. Throw your uppercut. Wipe away the perspiration. Recognize your true enemy. Call him out. Flip the script. Embrace Christ. Confess His power. Declare His glory. Sing of His salvation. Keep your chin up. Anticipate His rescue. Cling to His hand. Regain your strength. Claim your title. Walk in victory. Never look back.

More than anything, my brother, my sister, be assured that God is no respecter of persons. He does not play favorites. What He did for others, He will do for you. You may not know Jesus, but "the day you hear My voice," Jesus said, "harden not your heart." Jesus wants to come into your life. He wants to give your life structure and success. Just repeat this simple prayer, and be sincere in your heart:

> *"Lord, I'm sorry for all of my sins. I believe that You lived, that You died, and that You rose again, just for me. And God, I promise You, that from this day forward, I'm going to live a life that will make You proud. I promise, O God, to quit my sinful, evil ways and follow You. God, I thank You for another chance. In Jesus' Name. Amen.*

If you said that prayer, and meant every word in your heart, the Bible says, inextricably, that you are saved!

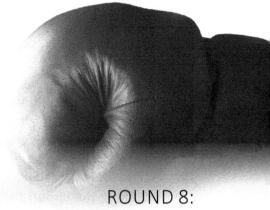

A BOUT WITH DOUBT

The alarm goes off. Time to get up. Time to pray. Time to supplicate and cry out unto God. Time to punctuate your morning sacrifice by turning to the Word. Pour a glass of freshly squeezed orange juice. Read and meditate upon your favorite Psalm. Then, of course, nothing can beat an early morning jog. While you are out, the sun is coming up. Stop for a second. Hold still. Look around. What do you see? There is nothing new under the sun. Whatever has occurred will occur again. Whatever has been done will be done again. Doubt will never go away until we send it away for good. Until then, we will wrestle with its coun- terparts which play out in every branch of our lives: During crisis, during episodes of guilt from our past mistakes, in the aftermath of verdicts which threaten our perception of justice and fairness, through the convenient escape of New Age reasoning, through the temptation of sin, the direct influence of close friends and the outspokenness of loved ones. These scenarios aimed at decep- tion, smudged across the pages of our memories, remain deeply imbedded into our senses, restraining the free exercise of our faith. How nice to be able to forget those moments when the brutal words of close friends cut to the core, leaving an unsightly wound. But we cannot forget it. Nor can we avoid the confusing message it sends to believers who are doing all they can to live for Christ.

Many of us are just barely holding on. *What we see* is constantly picking a fight with *what we know*. In the middle of the scuffle is the age-old question of why the righteous suffer and the wicked prosper. This is an ongoing issue which has not ceased to resonate. Today, the problem is re-enacted with even greater drama. The drama escalates with every succeeding generation: from doubting the importance of attending weekly worship to doubting the sanctity of marriage. To squash this snake in the grass, doubt, we must pull off the mask of denial and flatly admit that we have all been there. Before receiving Christ and after receiving Him, we have found ourselves wrestling erratically with doubt in multiple areas on multiple levels. How many times have you had to endure persecution, mistreatment, wrongdoing and downright exploitation while those inflicting the mistreatment seem to be thriving, prospering and flourishing, unchecked and undisciplined? God, however, had an answer for Habakkuk and He has an answer for you. He is neither indifferent nor inadequate; rather, He is on the field just when He seems most invisible. While listening to Habakkuk's complaint, the Lord is raising up a nation to be the rod of His chastening hand. Though for many months, years and perhaps even decades, you have been praying to God about your problem, your prayers are being heard and God is working things out for you while you are yet praying.

As is typical with international politics, Judah had a brief period of downtime while the balance of power was changing. But the days of Assyria were numbered. Babylon would soon be knocking on Judah's door with one purpose in mind—conquest. Habakkuk's description of the Chaldean army on the march is quite graphic. Not unlike today, it depicts a bitter, hasty nation with no regard for human life or social values. While this parade plays out, the Babylonians arrogantly glorify their own strength, performing repeated acts of unspeakable cruelty to accomplish their ungodly aims. Again, nothing new under the sun. This climate was affecting Habakkuk then, no less than it is affecting us today. Habakkuk is not happy. The Chaldeans are at it again. They represent the typical dominant personality. We all know one, or two. They are controlling, they know it, and they are rubbing it in. They like to throw their weight around. They are unapologetic and unashamed.

The moment of truth is imminent. National tensions are running high. Habakkuk's nerves are on edge. Inwardly, he is totally stressed out. No one is around to check his blood pressure. He is completely fed up. He has been double-crossed by the hypocritical symptoms which have aroused doubt one time too many. Do not get it twisted—though he is able to remain cool and composed, at this point it is perhaps best to stay out of his way. Now is not the time to become a nuisance. Surely, he is God's prophet, the hand of the Lord is upon him, he has been called, qualified and sent, but he is feeling some kind of way. He is ticking, and just one smart comment from any of those Chaldeans will push his button and set him off!

Then, at last, just when long-awaited relief seems at arm's reach–the Lord's answer–rather than helping Habakkuk, only intensifies his problem. How can a God of holiness permit His people, though disobedient, to be annihilated by a brutal and godless executioner? Hands down, Judah is sinful! That alone is woeful enough. But for God to use these monstrous Babylonians as His agent of punishment seems inconsistent with His holiness. It is confusing, adding insult to injury. Of course, as we saw in our earlier bout with the Chaldeans, unbelievers do not face such problems—at least not in the short-term. Only those who believe in the true and living God are confronted with the paradox of prosperous evildoers and suffering saints. Is there an answer?

Think back to verse one when Habakkuk determines to wait for an answer. He intends to stand at his watch to see what the Lord will say. The Lord instructs him to write the vision that will come to him so the people could read it, reminding him that its fulfillment will surely come in God's good time. And, my friends, that's what bothers us the most. This came up in Chapter One: We expect God to operate according to our timeline. When we ask Him to move, save and rescue, we want it done quick, fast and in a hurry. But because God sees the past, present and the future all at the same time, His divine perspective is far different from ours. While we are limited in what we can see, God's view is incomprehensible. We can only see what is, but God can see what was, what is, and what will be all at that same time. In other words, if you only see yourself being overwhelmed and swallowed up by your current situation, now is the time to take a harder look. If you do, you will see yourself coming out of your hopeless predicament. You will see yourself submitting to God's warm caring hands. You will see yourself being molded into a warrior, armed with the ammunition to handle your up-and-coming victory!

However, before you can claim your victory, you must survive the process of development. This is what each round in the ring has been all about: development. Every new move, upper cut, jab, hook, cross—is all about development. Only by working through this all-important process of development will you avoid the thrill of victory prematurely—that is, before you can handle it. It was during my own developmental stage that I learned to appreciate the vicissitudes of reality and celebrate the power of promise. But between reality and promise there is this great gap and the only way to progress from reality to the promise is to stretch yourself—to expand your faith. You must hold back nothing in affirming that God will bring you to what He has surely promised. I repeat, faith must be your bridge.

To cross that bridge safely, you must not become rattled by the portrayal of Babylon's destruction in Chapter 4, verses 4 – 19. God has not abdicated His moral character to pagan people. Not only will sin be punished, but sin will also punish itself. God has established a world so morally solid that history repeatedly testifies to the self-destructiveness of sin. Stay awake and pay close attention—We are not just punished for our sins, quite often we are punished by our sins. God will use Babylon as an instrument to chasten His people because He loves us. But the pagan king naturally will think his victory is by virtue of his own ability. Be not dismayed for one second: After God has used him to accomplish His purpose, God will discipline him and finally destroy him! Stay out of the way. You do *not* want to be anywhere around when this goes down. The only audible sounds will be cries of "woe!" They are within earshot of verses 6 through 19. These are "taunt songs" to the ones who glorify themselves in pride, ignoring the basic laws of morality. From the last verse of Chapter 2, a word arrives from God to Habakkuk. The prophet is left no choice than to recognize that God is in His holy temple working His sovereign will. The earth must trust Him and keep silent. The healthiest testimony that can surface from this position of silence is, "I do not understand it, but I trust you, God." History will conclude that Habakkuk was satisfied once he understood God's long-range plan.

At times, he may have felt like the poet who wrote:

I know there are no errors
In the great eternal plan;
And all things work together
For the final good of man.

Or another who wrote:

The world will never adjust itself
To suit your whims to the letter;
Some things will go wrong, your whole life long,
And the sooner you know it the better.

It's folly to fight with the infinite
And go down at last in the wrestle'
The wiser man shapes into God's plan
Like the water shapes into the vessel.

Habakkuk, at last, is bold, courageous and unwavering in His witness that God is alive and active despite external events which falsely indicate the opposite. For every desperate moment you spend in that ring, dancing about, throwing clever swings and savvy punches at doubt, guard this one fact in your sanctified mind: God *will* come through! Ultimately, character wins. Not always immediately, but in God's perfect timing, right always prevails. Knowing this, let us therefore not become weary in well doing, "for in due season we shall reap, if we faint not" (Galatians 6:9).

Habakkuk's brief prophecy closes with a lyrical outburst. His poem begins with vivid imagery, describing the Lord's wondrous works in the world. It concludes with a portrayal of the security and soaring power of those who live in intimate fellowship with God. Of course, Habakkuk must wait for full vindication, but he will do so quietly, confident in the integrity of God's government. Kyle Yates wrote, "Even though disaster and destruction await him, Habakkuk comes to realize that he can trust implicitly in his Lord."

What is Habakkuk's message for us? We should believe our beliefs and doubt our doubts, never making a skeptic's mistake of believing our doubts. Habakkuk's faith was fortified, and his insight was purified when he was willing to wait for God to answer him. God honors and rewards anyone who sincerely seeks the truth. He will not leave such a person hopeless and with unanswered questions. Time and again, it has become crystal clear that those who have access to true spiritual power are not those who have never entertained doubt. Rather, they are those who have examined their hearts honestly and faced their doubts candidly, emerging victoriously with a tender spirit and complete confidence. Such are those who are able to "Cleave ever to the sunnier side of doubt and cling to faith beyond the forms of faith." (Tennyson)

Habakkuk's experience tells us that we should not deny nor hide our doubts. Far less should we be ashamed of them. It will take eternity to understand infinity, but we can use our doubts and rise above them to higher concepts of God than we ever believed were possible. Ah yes! You can live an astoundingly happy life, if only you can fix your hopes on eternal things–if only you can believe.

So, my brothers and sisters, please understand, because you are a God-fearing, Spirit-filled believer, the enemy will absolutely, continually pick an ongoing fight with you. But remember God will never place any more upon you than you are able to bear. No matter your circumstance, the devil will always strive to stir up doubt within your heart. He wants to solidify your status as a doubter. Doubt is not, never has been and never will be on your side. He comes to steal, kill and destroy. But thanks be to God for His Word which promises, "If God be for us, who can be against us?" (Romans 8:31). The matter is already settled: When the enemy comes in like a flood, God will lift up a standard against them.

Speaking of the enemy, that old slimy devil tried to take my wife from me. That's when the gloves really came off. I will never forget it. When First Lady Karen was admitted to the hospital and had undergone surgery, she called to tell me to come pick her up because she was being discharged. I was on my way to the hospital and simply glad to bring her home. You have to know how I am when it comes to treating Karen when she is ill. She probably would say, and I will agree, that I overdo it, when it comes to attending to her hand and foot. As I was on my way to the hospital, I received a call informing me, "something has happened." At first I did not know what to think, but when I arrived at the hospital and I saw all of these doctors in her room, of course, I was alarmed and puzzled. That was one of the most difficult times in my life. It was during these moments that I wrote the song, "A Bout With Doubt." I also preached a sermon by the same title. It was a bout with doubt because the devil kept telling me that she was not going to make it. When the doctors came out and told me that 98% of the people who even approach her level of sickness do not make it, well of course, that was absolutely devastating.

I recall going to the hospital one night, she was comatose. The same night, when I left her room and walked out of the hospital, I looked straight up in the sky and I began to pray to God, "If this is the end for us, please take me and leave Karen." That was because I had made provisions for them to live without me and I felt that she would be better for the children. Of course, that was just absolutely a horrific experience. Then, the next day, I returned to the hospital with my mom, dad and brother. We went into the hospital chapel, and I can recall praying and just crying out to God. I recall seeing an image of God on the side of

A BOUT WITH DOUBT!

the chapel wall and God told me, "Didn't I tell you she would be alright?" That was when I got a breakthrough! The next day Karen came out of it. But it was a very frightening experience. It was indeed a bout with doubt, but God saw us through. My testimony is sure, that through it all, I have learned to trust in Jesus, I have learned to trust in God.

Beloved saints, please do not misinterpret the path that I take by the prestige of the gold chain around my neck nor the symbolism of my ring. Please believe me, I have had my share of dark days and long, stormy nights. I do not have all of the answers and now is a good time for you also to shake off that pressure of thinking that *you* need to have all the answers. Over the years, as a student, a minister, a pastor, a husband, father, grandfather, Prelate and even a Presiding Bishop, I have learned one of the wisest things I can say is "I don't know."

However, my brothers and sisters, there is one thing that *I do* know. There is no time more pressing than right now for you to make up your mind to trust in Jesus, to trust in God, to trust His Word, to trust His holiness, to trust his love. There is no time more pressing that right now to arise and personify the very name of Habakkuk by "embracing" your job description:

Prerequisites: While God does not discriminate on the basis of race, color, ethnic or cultural persuasion, the fact remains, "they that wait upon the Lord shall renew their strength; they shall mount up with wings as eagles; they shall run, and not be weary; and they shall walk, and not faint." Similarly, it is not quite enough to wait on the Lord, but you must wait on the Lord and be of good courage. He will strengthen your heart. Only a strong heart can endure doubt's antagonizing pushes and punches.

Days/Hours: There will be seasons when you will have to work, worship and serve with cuts, bruises, scrapes, scratches and deep painful wounds that do not heal overnight. Nevertheless, from the rising of the sun unto the going down of the same the LORD'S name is to be praised. Because at the end of the day, "the just shall live by faith."

Job Description: To cast the devil out of the mind. To walk not in the counsel of the ungodly. To stand not in the way of sinners.

102

To not sit in the seat of the scornful. But to delight in the law of the Lord; mediate upon it day and night.

Benefits Package: You will be like a tree planted beside the rivers of water. You will bring forth fruit in your season. Your leaf will not wither. And whatever you do will prosper!

Successful Background Check: For the Lord knoweth the way of the righteous. But the way of the ungodly–Chaldeans and all– will perish. In fact, He knows the way that you take; and when He has tried you—you shall come forth as gold.

Office Skills: The ability to declare, word for word:

I'm pressing on the upward way,
New heights I'm gaining every day;
Still praying as I'm onward bound,
"Lord, plant my feet on higher ground."

Lord, lift me up, and let me stand
By faith on heaven's tableland;
A higher plane than I have found,
Lord, plant my feet on higher ground.

If you can just stay planted, if you can stay in the ring, then you can stay up in doubt's face. If you can stay in doubt's face, you can stay in the race. Never mind those who have already written you off or counted you out–because, when all is said and done, those who have counted you out, can't count!

REFERENCES

The Art of Decision-Making. (2021). Psychology Today. https://www.psychologytoday.com

21st Century King James Version Bible. www.biblegateway.com.

C. Alan Anderson And Deborah G. Whitehouse. *New Thought: A Practical American Spirituality.* New York, NY, Crossroad Publishing Company, 1995.

"Cross-modal induction of thalamocortical potentiation leads to enhanced information processing in the auditory cortex," Emily Petrus, Amal Isaiah, Adam P. Jones, David Li, Hui Wang, Hey-Kyoung Lee and Patrick O. Kanold, was published Feb. 5, 2014 in *Neuron*.

English Standard Version Bible. (2021). English Standard Version Bible. https://www.biblegateway.com

Habakkuk's Song of Thanksgiving in Time of Calamity. (2010). Christian Library. https://www.christian-studylibrary.org/article/habakkuk%E2%80%99s-song- thanksgiving-time-calamity

How to Make Peace with Your Past. (2020). Psychology Today. https://www.psychologytoday.com

In America, Does More Education Equal Less Religion? (2017). Pew Research Center. https://www.pewresearch.org/

King James Version Bible. www.biblegateway.com. McNulty, F. (1980). The Burning Bed (1st ed.). Harcourt.

The Message Bible. (2021). The Message Bible. https://www. gateway.com Murray, W. J. (2012). My Life Without God (Classics) (1st ed.). WND Books.

National Mental Health Consumer and Carer Forum (NMHCCF) Advocacy Brief Issue: Consumer and Carer Participation – Key Issues and Benefits (2010) https://nmhccf.org.au/sites/ default/files/docs/final_cc_participation.pdf

New American Standard Version Bible. www.biblegateway.com.

New Century Version Bible. (2021). New Century Version Bible. https://www.biblegateway.com

Questions and Answers. (2021).

1918%20Pandemic%20(H1N1%20virus)%20_%20 Pandemic%20Influenza%20(Flu)%20_%20CDC.Html. https:// www.cdc.gov/flu/pandemic-resources/basics/faq.html

Sheir, Rebecca. "Gallaudet Finds Deaf People Don't See Better, They See Differently."

WAMU 88.5 | AMERICAN UNIVERSITY RADIO, wamu.org/ story/11/06/28/gallaudet_finds_deaf_people_dont_see_ better_they_see_dif ferently.

"The Implications of COVID-19 for Mental Health and Substance Use." *KFF,* 2021, www.kff.org/coronavirus-covid-19/issue-brief/the-implications-of-covid-19-for- mental-health-and-substance-use.

"Teen Brain: Behavior, Problem Solving, and Decision Making." *American Academy of Child and Adolescent Psychiatry.,* 2016, www.aacap.org/AACAP/Families_and_Youth/Facts_ for_Families/FFF-Guide/The- Teen-Brain-Behavior-Problem-Solving-and-Decision-Making-095.aspx.

REFERENCES

Tigar, Lindsay. "The 101 Guide to Boxing Terminology and Techniques." *Aaptiv*, aaptiv.com/magazine/boxing-terminology.

What is Validation and Why Do I Need to Know? (2012). PsychCentral. https://psychcentral.com/

Who were the Chaldeans in the Bible? (2021). Who Were the Chaldeans in the Bible? https://www.biblegateway.com

"Why Didn't You Say Anything?" (2020, September 20). The Hotline. https://www.thehotline.org/resources/why-didnt-you-say-anything/

CPSIA information can be obtained
at www.ICGtesting.com
Printed in the USA
BVHW050713160723
667307BV00005B/149